Fill the Room

An Invitation to Take Up Space

Joyce Parry Moore

Tehom Center Publishing is a 501(c)3 nonprofit publishing feminist and queer authors, with a commitment to elevate BIPOC writers.

Paperback ISBN: 978-1-966655-60-2

Ebook ISBN: 978-1-966655-61-9

Contents

Dedicated to Ari, who fills our hearts and leads the way

Acknowledgments

Writing and publishing a book is something akin to giving birth. And many births are facilitated by a team of supporters, in which I have been most fortunate.

First, I thank my "book doula," the Rev. Dr. Angela Yarber, whose publishing company, Tehom Center Publishing, lifts up and amplifies marginalized writing. Special thanks to my thoughtful editor, Diana McLean, for clarifying my voice without stifling it. I've also been supported during much of my journey–before, during, and after the birth of this volume–by my own coaches, the Rev. Dr. Scott Stoner, and consultant Hannah Mello and her team at Cambio for Growth. My counselor, Laura Moon Williams, has helped me heal from so many traumas and regain my resilience. And to my beautiful, creative, loving friends who've put up with me for years and who daily inspire me to keep on keeping on–endless thanks.

Finally, deepest gratitude to my husband, Patrick, and my grown children, and growing grandchildren, in our blended family (shaken, not stirred). You are my beginning and my ending. You fill my life and make it possible for me to show up in the world. Thank you.

A few words about my words

There are a few stylized terms I use throughout the book that might benefit from a little explanation at the get go.

First, I tend toward saying "human" instead of "person," a trend loaned to me by younger and queer colleagues. Saying "human" feels more inclusive to me, and makes space for embracing individual qualities, sometimes creating an alternative to other, more gendered words.

I also use the spelling "folx," rather than folks, another method of conveying greater inclusion, especially for nonbinary humans. I invite you to consider trying this spelling yourself, or simply translate for your comfort level.

Finally, you'll see the spelling "G*d" used throughout the book, except when I am directly quoting another speaker. To begin with, the Hebrew language does not contain vowels, only vowel pointings; additionally they do not generally write the name of the Divine. This spelling reminds me that no one culture or gender expression lays an exclusive claim to the divine. I encourage you to translate this spelling into whatever word conveys the ineffable for you.

Also, you'll find a number of exercises throughout the book, indented to set them apart. You can try these while you're reading or find them again on my website at joyceparrymoore.com where they're recorded for a deeper, hands free experience.

Now, read on. We've got places to go, my humans.

Prelude

Prelude: An introductory performance, action, or event preceding and preparing for an important matter; a musical section or movement introducing the theme.

One person plus one typewriter constitutes a movement.

— Pauli Murray, first transgender Episcopal
clergy-human

IT WAS TIME.

After years and years of gritting her teeth, pressing her lips together; of playing small and fitting in, of stepping back, taking the high road, not making too much noise, or upsetting anyone, or taking up too much space; of swallowing insults and enduring injuries to herself and to others, others with closed mouths and frightened eyes; years of apologizing like it was her job, of depre-

cating herself into acceptable oblivion, of shrinking into corners, or seeking some small spot at the table where she would try on occasion to be heard, only to find herself ignored, overlooked, invisible.

After countless, countless cuts, bruises, and burns crisscrossing her skin, her soul, her story, in a lifelong pattern of oppression, abuse, and survival. After witnessing, again–AGAIN–a brilliant, qualified, capable public servant–a woman–diminished and passed over for an ignorant, arrogant, male icon of misogyny and racism, an actual criminal–worse, sexual predator–after feeling her own wounds open, bloodying her scars anew, after ALL THAT, she'd had enough. Fucking more than enough. She said "when."

Even her chosen profession, her calling, which she entered with her whole heart, wanting to make a difference in people's lives and in the world, teemed with misogyny. Her heart ached from the most recent betrayal, after she dared to step forward as her full self. Punished again for speaking out, for speaking up, for advocating for herself and others on the margins. Expelled from the system that she sought to impact and transform, shunned for standing her ground.

Shame circled her like carrion, waiting to feed on her insecurities and disappointment. Why couldn't she fix this? It must be her fault. She'd brought all of herself into this vocation: her creativity, her caring, her innovation, and her entrepreneurial spirit. No matter what she tried, she simply didn't fit. Was she too much? Not enough? It was hard to tell.

Her body continued to fold in on itself; her stomach tightened every time she even drove toward that place, as she tried to shrink herself to fit, to humble her unruly spirit. Every day, she felt a part of herself fade away, disappear, die. That was good, right? Weren't we supposed to die to our "selves" to be of more service? She wondered, though, who did that benefit?

When she thought of those who had used their power and influence to shut her out, she didn't see humility or compassion. She saw a colonizing obedience to a system that excluded the voices of the *very people whom it claimed to serve—women, people of color, queer folx, people with disabilities. Those who had ignited the very start of the spiritual movement she vowed to follow, now either fled from the institution to save their dignity, or stayed away because they, like her, simply did not fit the "norm."*

Alone now, abandoned by the institution to which she'd given so much of her life, she struggled to sleep, to breathe, to dream. Night after night, she asked the darkness for answers: what would she do now? Who would she become? What did she want?

She stilled her breath and remembered countless times when the room around her, defying stifling expectations, nonetheless filled with love and light, with hope and inspiration. She thought of the inexpressible joy she experienced when her voice connected with others—singing, speaking, writing, advising—and she thought, maybe it wasn't her that didn't fit. Perhaps the institution itself had failed her, as it had failed so many. Its narrow traditions, its fear-driven focus on sustaining itself at all costs, in the end had made it too small, too little for her.

She felt so foolish: why had she ignored this truth for so long? Why had she returned, time and time again, giving more of her energy, passion, and resources only to be knocked down and out by those with so little imagination and vision? Was this now a final chapter in her journey to release the patterns of abuse that had plagued and limited the first half of her life?

Despite everything, she still believed that, in an abundant universe, nothing was ever truly wasted. She'd done good, seen transformations in people's lives. She'd poked some holes in the toxic fabric and let in just a little bit of light. Maybe that would bring some healing, eventually.

She thought of all of her life adventures, all that she'd been privileged to see and do. Some hard things too, some painful challenges. She could do that again. Damn right she could! And as she realized this, the light began to return to the center of her chest. She unfolded, and her flame, that had by now dwindled down to a mere glowing ember, rekindled and sparked.

She could hear all the voices of those who'd come to her over the years of her life, seeking health and encouragement. Seeking their truth and their path. Those years of sacrifice and education had also taught her many new skills and brought her more healing of past traumas. Now she could be free to share with those seekers, those who would never enter the walls of the box that had so recently expelled her. She would go to them. She would stretch her own voice, her words, her love and light, and connect with a much broader community. With those whose voices had, like hers, been sidelined and stymied.

Together, they would create another movement, one that could break down walls of colonialism and oppression, that would release and empower so many voices that a shift might truly become possible. A shift in vibration, in values, in power, in the spaces where decisions were made and stories were told. Together they would fill those spaces unapologetically, with integrity and confidence. But first, she had to get out of bed.

She rose up slowly and put her feet firmly on the floor, wiggling her toes to feel her connection to the earth. Sleep clouding her weary eyes, she parted her cracked lips, bared her teeth, stretched her aching arms wide, wider, stood tall, to her full height; she took a deep breath and roared!

The Movement is You

You have been told that your voice–singing, speaking, writing, creating–must be accepted by experts to matter. You've been told that you must disappear into the collective for your voice to have virtue. The truth I tell you today is that you can achieve powerful personal and communal transformation by finding, healing, developing, and sharing your own, unique voice and *Filling the Room* in a big way.

How often have you been told to "tone it down," be smaller, quieter, less contrary? To not "be so sensitive" or "make a big deal" out of something?

"Don't be so political!" we were cautioned. How did we reply? Did we quote second wave feminist Carol Hanish and assert, "The personal *is* political"?

How many times a day do we–those who identify as feminists, LGBTQIA+ humans, and/or black, Indigenous, and people of color (BIPOC)–receive subtle and not-so-subtle messages suggesting that we shrink: in our bodies, our voices, our ideas, our presence? In how many ways do we trap ourselves with the subliminal (or not) warning that to stand out, to reach our full stature and expression, may pose a very real danger to us and those like us? Could it be because our creativity threatens those in control?

Take a moment right now and recall just one of the (I'm sure many) times you've been in a meeting or conversation, and had your idea, your voice, go unheard, only later to hear your thoughts repeated by a (likely) straight, white male to great acclaim? Or how about when you were told that your voice was too "shrill," or that someone could not *hear* what you had to say because of its register or "accent"?

Does the very thought of "filling the room" fill you with guilt? Did you hesitate before picking up and opening this book? You may ask yourself, as you have been conditioned to think, "who am I to take up so much space? What about other people? Won't it diminish them?" To be clear, we're not talking about dominating conversations, or becoming a narcissist. What we're about here is *showing up* for the conversation as our complete selves, with our unapologetic voices, and amplifying other such voices even if (especially if) it goes against the "norm."

Despite everything, I believe this much to be true: there is room for all of us. Like so many pursuits of justice–human rights, housing and food security, diversity–showing up as our full and authentic selves *is not a zero-sum game*. I'm here to tell you what I've learned: that you have the right and the room and the invitation to take up all the space you need and to show up with your full, powerful voice. Are you ready to say "when"? To throw off the straitjacket of false narratives and become the person you've dreamt of? To write your own narrative and roar?

I'm so glad you're here. It's going to be okay. Better than okay. It's going to be expansive, powerful, resistant. You're going to bubble over and rise up to your full stature. This journey will connect you to yourself, to the Divine (as you understand her), and to other creative, transcendent creatures. You are supported by me, by other like-hearted voices, and by the universe we're co-creating together. Together, we reflect the fabulous, feisty dream of a world based on compassion, inclusion, and possibility, shining in today's context of fear, oppression, and tiny, false narratives.

I know you may feel afraid right now, looking over your shoulder, worried about pissing off those in power. Good. Let's learn to speak to that fear, and transform it from an energy that denies, and shrinks, and controls to one that expands, vibrates, and propels us forward. Are you with me? All right, my lovelies, let's go!

So, how's all this going to happen?

Fill the Room coaching–vocal, living, and spiritual–offers you unique insights, exercises, and accompaniment on this journey. I've been there myself; I'm persisting every day, and I'm delighted and honored to help guide you on your journey. You may be asking (as I do, on the regular) "who are you to advise/accompany/support me on such a journey?" Good question.

I'm a scholar of creative arts, theology, and counseling with decades of experience under my sequined belt, and I'm more than happy to nerd out with you at any time about Mozart, Brecht, Thurman, Rogers, and more. I'm an ordained (and retired) Episcopal priest, and certified as a life coach, with a doctorate in pastoral counseling. I'm a mom, stepmom, nanna, and opera singer (as one is), who's lived in Washington, Boston, New York, Alaska (yup), California, and British Columbia, Canada. As a trained and seasoned performing artist, voice teacher, spiritual leader, and counselor, I've participated first-hand across cultures, races, and abilities, across genders and orientations and generations, in the strength and beauty available to each human when they discover and celebrate their own authentic voice and story.

Today's dominant culture of comparison tries to convince us that there is only one correct standard of beauty and authenticity, and that if we don't measure up to that definition, we have no voice at all. That dominant culture wants us to believe this nonsense, and for a long time I did believe it. No shame if you have too. I'm here today telling you that it is a false and limiting mindset, one designed primarily to preserve a system that benefits the privileged few. As a white, straight woman, I know that I benefit on some levels from that system. And when I speak out as a feminist, ally, and anti-racist liberation theologian, I'm honored to forfeit some of that privilege.

Here's what I've seen: time and again, I've witnessed and facilitated the amazing personal transformations that blossom when we give ourselves and one another the permission and practices to strengthen our own voices. You may have been told to blend, to disappear, to step so far back that you don't remember who you are anymore. But here's what I think: until you receive the encouragement and space to develop and cherish your own expression, your own unique and delightful message, you cannot collaborate in a meaningful solidarity. We were not created to disappear, but to shine, and then to shine together. We're here to complement one another, to challenge one another into fullness, not to blend ourselves into extinction.

I also deeply believe in the power of joining strong voices together for common causes. Yet to do so in innovative and groundbreaking systems, we must come together in ways that are not colonizing or diminishing, but rather honoring and supporting, so that each voice, each life, each soul can bring their full and authentic selves and contribute (or not contribute) to the whole. That's a tall order, I know. We've been colonized, and colonizing, for so long that it's honestly hard to imagine a new way, and we must be vigilant for the trappings of those false and demanding "norms" creeping in on us. Yet, as adrienne maree brown suggests in *Emergent Strategy,* more than one way is possible and even advisable:

> We have to create futures in which everyone doesn't have to be the same kind of person...I want an interdependence of lots of kinds of people with lots of belief systems, *and* continual evolution.[1]
>
> Creating more possibilities counters the very foundational assumptions about strategy...a military term, which means a [single] plan of action...a practice of narrowing down, identifying one path forward, one way...[2]

As many of my faithful friends of color have taught me, I believe that the Divine makes a way from no way. And we are called to co-create that new way.

That's why I'm writing this book. The world needs the voices of loud women, bold queer folx, resilient BIPOC, and innovative creatives of diverse neuro and physical abilities, unafraid to take

---

1. brown, adrienne maree, *Emergent Strategies,* pg. 57
2. Ibid, pg. 155

up all the space we need. We cannot continue to stay small while the world, the planet, suffers and dies at the call of bullying, misogynist voices intent on running things and on locking everyone else in little boxes. I don't know about you, but I'm sick to the teeth of boxes.

This is the time for us to break out: with our singing, speaking, writing; with leading and creating and reforming. Our combined voices can and will and must make the walls of oppression fall. As with the walls of Jericho (only without the colonizing of Indigenous cultures), can we march around and blow our horns loud and long enough to bust shit up?

Now, more than perhaps any other time in our history, there exists an urgent need to lift up marginalized voices, including our own. *Fill the Room* coaching offers wisdom, practices, and community to support you, and us, to do just that. Individual coaching and mentoring in voice–physically, metaphorically, and creatively–provides one foundation for growing confidence and skill in expression and personal integrity. Life coaching, with or without vocal instruction, accompanies that journey toward self-discovery and channels personal passion and expression toward impactful goals. Spiritual coaching, with or without the context of any faith tradition, grounds these practices by helping you delve into important questions of identity and purpose. Finally, group endeavors–workshops, retreats, and other creative projects–encourage you to find a "choir" of other voices who share your passions–your people–and to join to make communal and systemic transformation. Rinse and repeat. It's a process, and when we get exhausted, even resting can be resistant, and we can trust our allies to continue to sing.

How did I get here?

For years of my life, being raised in a patriarchal family of origin, I absorbed messages of fear and misogyny pertaining to my gender. Images in movies, television, or books, of women becoming the object of derision or even violence due to their "voices"–their ways of showing up and expressing themselves in the world.

In the '60s, when my childhood awareness of the world around me developed, women began emerging as the central characters in television series. Still, any power that they possessed had to be offset by their goofy antics, along with their male-approved beauty. Marlo Thomas capered through New York city as *That Girl*, her modern ideas offset by constant kooky mishaps; Barbara Eden wore a midriff baring, sheer harem costume as the genie in, *I Dream Of Jeannie*, and her power to make actual magic (I may have practiced her crossed-armed head nod) still able to be contained in a bottle by her "master." Ditto with Samantha, the "good witch" on *Bewitched* (yes, I practiced her nose twitch too) who could perform amazing feats and set everything right, only if she had dinner on the table for her mortal husband. Message received!

My own mother, uneducated and having survived a traumatic childhood with alcoholic parents, continued to suffer at the hands of my father whenever she spoke too loudly, argued, or even drew attention to her ample bosom by what she wore. Without an example of nurturing to emulate, Mom found herself unequipped to become a mother to even one, let alone two children. As the eldest, and yet not a male child, I was "too much" for her. Even after my dad's early death, momma would often catch herself saying something he might have considered too outspoken, and cautioned herself under her breath, muttering "Shut up, Sally!" She believed she was "too much," as well, and passed that legacy along to me.

Small wonder, perhaps, that I found beauty, freedom, and even safety in my young adulthood in an unconventional setting: the operatic stage. While studying to command a courtroom or legislative body seemed far too risky for me, requiring me to "out" my intellect and face danger, I felt safe and at home while singing for hundreds. Surely, no one would tell me to "shut up" there? Enter the world of western European classical music, controlled by (you guessed it) white men. There are plenty of limitations there to navigate.

In the second half of my vocal career, I began teaching voice lessons. It's what you do. I started off when I moved to Juneau, Alaska, where I worked for a regional theatre and eventually founded my own company. Juneau is a magical place, full of natural beauty and creative people. A place where I rediscovered my artist's heart and my true voice.

My clients came from many demographics: high school students, many of whom desired to go on and study music and performance in college and beyond; a handful of local performers of all genders; singers and actors, who wanted to improve their technique and get over their jitters; and many mature women who sought something else, something they couldn't yet articulate.

This last group often came to me focusing on some short-term goal–a choir concert, a wedding or church service–with a larger, deeper yearning hidden beneath. Especially among this group, tears happened. Not because I'm mean (which I'm not) or because they were unstable (we all are), but tears flowed when they discovered something in themselves–perhaps an unheard sound, so big they could not ignore it, so big that it began to dispel all those negative messages they'd received over the years. They came face to face with those voices, or "gremlins" I call them, and dared to challenge what they'd been told. They cried with relief, with grief, and with power.

One client, a slight, shy woman in her 50s, struggled to rediscover her head voice after years of speaking in a forced lower tone in a vain effort to be taken seriously. Her laughter gave away her true nature: light and sparkling, filling her eyes and the room around her. We worked patiently for months, seeking the confidence to connect with that natural part of her voice. Then one afternoon as we sang an Italian art song, she emitted a sound so free and soaring that it surprised both of us.

"Oh my!" she exclaimed, eyes wide. "Did that come out of me?"

Then she began to weep, and laugh, and we paused to acknowledge the magnitude of what had just happened.

Weeks later, she purchased a used piano and started practicing at home in the morning. She finally retired from a job she hated, and joined a choir as a soprano. She was on her way!

In those days, before my training as a counselor, coach, and pastor, I still knew enough to honor those moments as holy. I would pause, give space, acknowledge the feelings. Then I had to recommend that they take these thoughts to a counselor or coach, and we proceeded with the music.

As I matured, and developed further during my journeys of motherhood and then breast cancer, I was drawn from the stage to the altar and went off to seminary. Even in the stained-glass atmosphere of the Church, I experienced the real danger for feminists all around me: in the classroom, the pulpit, the board room. As I struggled to somehow realize my true self in a package small and non-offensive enough to escape abuse, and yet loud enough to make a difference, I found that I'd had enough. I realized I *was* enough.

Throughout this blessed adventure around the world, I gathered pieces to my own puzzle and gained the wisdom and compassion I would eventually bring full circle. Here. Now. To you.

What's your story? If you drew a map of your journey thus far, what would it look like? What gifts and wisdom have you earned along the way that you bring to our collaboration, today?

This Roadmap

In this book I will offer you the awareness, skills, and inspiration to liberate your voice, reigniting your confidence to expand beyond repression. As a feminist, BIPOC, trans or queer human you have the right to take up space with your stories, ideas, creations, and solutions–to explode with fierce beauty, sound, and light. To fill the room, the concert hall, the theatre, the street, the floors of Congress, you name it. The planet urgently needs the kind of transformations made possible only through the revolutionary power of our combined resonance. I want to hear you; we need to hear you. Let it out! Your screams, laughter, your whoops and hollers, high notes and low notes, your dances and battles-- they all point the way.

In the following three chapters, we'll experience three movements in the continuing cycle of discovering, developing, and connecting to others with our voices. "Movement" here conveys a double meaning: both a shift in cultural norms, forwarded in this case by voices previously relegated to the margins, to the wings, as it were; and the term as used in musical composition.

One standard structure in classic, European compositions is "sonata form." It consists of three movements: the exposition, which we'll think of as Discovery of the central theme; the Development of that theme; and the recapitulation, Connecting the original theme to the development of the entire piece and beyond.

As we consider sonata form–either as a new concept or in a new light–you might treat yourself by listening to one or more sublime compositions in that structure. Here are some suggestions:

- The Bach cello Sonata in BMinor;
- any of Mozart's many sonatas for violin and piano;
- believe it or not, sonatas by women (!) like Ellen Taaffe Zwilich, the first woman to receive her doctorate in composition from New York's Juilliard School, who wrote a haunting sonata in three movements for violin and piano in 1974;
- if you hanker for a more brutal and angry composition, listen to Ruth Crawford-Seeger's violin sonata, written in 1926;
- Queer composers? Try one of Francis Poulenc's flute sonatas;
- And just when you thought that all composers are dead, check out the groundbreaking compositions of Jamaican British composer, conductor and violinist Shirley J. Thompson, who's still alive and shaking things up in the world of "classical" music.

Forms were made to be bent, broken, and reimagined. Thompson inspires us when she says, "As an artist you have to have a vision and in ways I have acted on the visions I've had for a very long time...I created the doors and opened them."

What doors shall we open together?

In the first movement of this book journey, our Discovery, we'll consider a broad definition of "voice" and how it relates to our vocation, our calling in life. We'll explore ways to listen for the sound of our identity. We'll affirm the power of that voice and embrace the fact that even one voice in a room can illuminate that space.

In the second movement, our Development section, we'll examine ways our voices can be healed from previous harm, both physically and emotionally. You'll have the chance to confront some of the false messages that forced you to play small, to be quiet, to sound and look like anyone other than who you were created to be. Using the metaphor and physical reality of vocal practice, we will introduce exercises to help you rediscover, strengthen, and heal your unique expression.

In our third movement, on Connection, we'll celebrate the possibility of liberating our voices, not only individually but collectively. We'll consider our sources of connection, even across cultures, in the face of heterosexist, colonizing, and racist dominance. We'll find our path to joining other marginalized voices in solidarity, without diminishing or colonizing any of us.

A brief trigger warning here: the book discusses abuse, both physical and emotional (though not in any detail), and mentions eating disorders and depression. If any of these topics make you anxious, take things gently, and feel free to skip ahead through troubling sections if needs be.

Since I'm writing a book about healing, developing, and sharing our narratives, I've included vignettes from my own life. No, I'm not trying to convince you to become an opera singer, or a priest, or to move to Alaska. (Although, if that's your jam, then go for it!) I do believe that every story, every fulsome discipline or journey of discovery, offers metaphors and lessons that can apply to other lives and pursuits. I warmly invite you to enter my stories, to take what you need, and leave the rest.

Each of our Movements also includes a personal story from a client and friend whom I've known for years, whose journey of self-discovery, development, and collaboration continues and can be traced in some way to finding their voice. These people are extraordinary, ordinary humans like you, using their voices not necessarily on any global stage, but to power a life of integrity and action. You, my beloved rebel, embody that same potential in your own way, following your own calling. Yes, I said "calling."

Inspiration belongs to and should be accessible for all of us, not just a select few, who adhere to some kind of pre-ordained standard, in some accepted format. Each of us harbors within our soul the potential to both inspire and be inspired, to create and to collaborate. The world, right now, needs us to believe that together. Especially for marginalized voices, as change-makers and survivors, we often shoulder the burden of cultural biases, generational traumas, and institutional expectations. I'm fucking done with letting it define who I am, how I feel, and what I do in the world. To quote the divine Ru Paul, "can I get an amen?!"

Together, let's discover new shapes, sounds, and structures with the possibility to change the song, the symphony, the method of composition. We'll fill the room with inspiration for a world longing to hear something other than a thoughtless worship of dominant voices. Ready? I know you are. I can hear you roar!

First Movement: Discover

There is in you something that waits and listens for the sound of the genuine in yourself and sometimes there is so much traffic going on in your mind. . . and in the midst of all of this you have got to find out what your name is. Who are you? How does the sound of the genuine come through to you...

— Howard Thurman, 1980 address to Spellman College

The Lightsaber

HE RUSHED UP TO ME DURING MORNING DROP OFF AT NORTHERN Lights Preschool, my most vulnerable time of the day. Every day by this point, it felt as though I'd already run a marathon. Now here I was, hastily wiping last night's mascara away from under my eyes, picking at my sweatshirt to hide my bralessness. I straightened up and tried to remember the name of this fellow parent. He confronted me before I could even remember to smile.

"I thought I knew you!" he blurted out, almost accusing.

"Um, are we sure about that?" I mumbled and he pressed on.

"Sorry. I'm Jimmy's dad. Hi. You see, I went to the symphony concert on Saturday night, and I heard you. Singing! Opera!! It was like realizing that someone you see every day was carrying around a lightsaber with them all this time!" He looked at me quizzically, waiting for some response. He'd have to wait.

A lightsaber, I thought; I'll take that. Singing–writing, painting, dancing, litigating–can feel at times like a superpower, like a very bright light, able to cut through the pretense, the expectations, the bullshit of everyday life. It doesn't matter whether you're getting paid to use this power. It's always amazing and surprising.

That weekend's concert was my first singing gig in a long while, at least since I'd given birth to our littlest one, Ari. Most people these days just thought of me as "Ari's Mom," and that was ok with me. I'd come to this Alaskan town to get away: away from the relentless push of New York City, away from my former marriage, away from who I thought I was and toward who I might really become. Here, thousands of miles away from that former identity, I'd sought the space to rediscover my voice, my song, to listen in the mountains and forests for the sound of my true voice.

Now I was stuck, again, having to explain that identity to another man. He was wrong: he had never really known me, still didn't. I wasn't prepared at 8:00 on Monday morning to figure it all out for him. I crossed my arms in front of my sweaty tits and questioned, "So, how do you feel about me now?" Pause.

Ball back in his court. What had he expected? Did he not realize that hearing a Mozart aria (Italian for song) might just change him? Did he not realize that so, so many of us, so many women, hid our superpowers every single day? What would he do now that his eyes opened?

"Well," he scratched his stubbly, Alaskan chin, "I guess it

makes me think of you with more respect. I mean, wow! If you're capable of that, then what else can you do?"

Ironically the aria I'd chosen for the concert was one of apology: in "Per pieta," from Cosi Fan Tutte, Mozart's soprano surmounted two challenges. First, begging forgiveness from her distant beau for cheating on him with his mustache-disguised friend (which, in opera, makes someone completely unrecognizable), a tenor who'd tested her faithfulness on a bet (you can't make these things up). Meanwhile, she sang some of the most impossibly florid and broad ranged (from high C to low G) vocal passages ever written. (Legend has it that Mozart had it in for the first soprano to sing that role!) With an orchestra. No way would I be apologizing again. He'd have to work this out.

"Sounds like you've got some thinking to do," I began, having to raise my voice over the growing chaos of the preschoolers greeting one another and starting to play.

"I guess we all have some hidden powers, hidden stories," I softened. Per pieta.

"Maybe from here on out, you can remember that and respect everyone a bit more? I don't know. Right now, I need coffee. See you later!" and I flounced out of the church building, as much as I could in sneakers and jeans.

In the safety of my minivan, I considered: maybe now was the time to stop hiding my lightsaber. The dream of starting an Alaskan touring opera company, with the name "Opera TO GO!" had hounded me long enough. It was time to act. To travel around the state and flash a team of lights all over the place–ZZZZipppp, ZZZZappp, ZZZopp–even remote locations. We'd go on ferries, on buses, on trucks, and on planes; we would fill rooms in schools, museums, concert halls, and gymnasiums. We'd make other people think and dream.

But for now, coffee. And maybe a shower.

Embracing Your Power

To this day, twenty years later, people share memories with me about our Alaskan musical adventures. People from our little capital town of Juneau, and professionals from around the country, who came to experience a sound of the genuine amidst the clang of a capitalist grind. Experiences that taught them, deep in their bones, that anything was possible. That their voices mattered. That they–that we–had hidden power. It made them consider how to use theirs.

Do you realize that you have a powerful voice? In whatever way you express it–in sound, or image, or written words–your voice carries the power to move others, to change things, to shake stuff up. You may have been conditioned to think of power as a negative thing, synonymous with the *abuse* of power. But power itself is not evil. It is the human agency that gives us tools for survival. Human agency that belongs to all of us. To deny or suppress that power to dominate any one person or group: that's oppression.

Your agency, your power, is important, perhaps more than you know. Right now, we need you to use it for your and our common good. But first, you need to make peace with your power.

In training for community organizing, one of the first things they taught is to reframe the term "power." Power, in their simplest definition, is "the ability to act." The ability to act. Nothing scary about that. Right?

Then we worked together to develop skills in ourselves and our colleagues: the ability to speak clearly and to listen deeply; the ability to advocate beside other folx without controlling them; the ability to connect people and resources and focus them on a common cause. One of the greatest tools was story: telling ours, hearing others'.

Here's how we practiced that. In organizing, we relied on what we called one-to-ones: extended conversations with colleagues where we asked questions that drew out their deep and genuine story, which we respectfully witnessed, and then shared our own with honesty and vulnerability. In this way, we began to listen ourselves and others into wholeness. Into solidarity.

You can start practicing this today; maybe you already do. Consider scheduling one-to-ones with, say, five people with whom you work, create, are in community. It's best to set clear parameters: 20 minutes for each person, with additional time for clarifying questions and future planning, for a total of one hour. This is best done in person if possible.

Here's what I believe: storytelling and listening can (and do) change the world. It's how we learn to hear the sound of the genuine. If I were to describe what I do, what I've done during my full lifetime, from stage to altar to studio, it is storytelling.

In *What's the Story*, her book of essays on art, theatre and cultural change, director Anne Bogart explores the way in which telling and witnessing stories changes both the teller and the listener. Bogart views and practices the art of theatre through the lens of the Brazilian founder of Theatre of Oppressed, Augusto Boal, who said, "Theater is a form of knowledge; it should and can also be a means of transforming society. Theater can help us build our future, rather than just waiting for it." (Bogart, pg. 10)

Whether in theatre or in life, Bogart theorizes that as humans, everything we do tells a story: our expressions, our energy, our posture, our actions. She connects to contemporary neuroscience that now proves how the very act of hearing or telling a story can change the structure of our brains. She encourages us to cultivate mindfulness around our narratives to gain greater agency in our lives.

Stories are one of the few aspects of our lives that, with a certain attentive will, we can control. It is possible to compose our own stories. We can choose how to outline and narrate the events that happen to us and the narratives that we devise can help prevent us from becoming powerless. But the option to take responsibility for our own stories requires effort, vigilance and accountability.

Not only that, but stories also focus that power, through communal meaning-making for which we all hunger as humans, to shift the structure and values of a society. In this regard, artists (which I contend we all have the possibility to become) take up the sacred calling to shape and care for the stories that we tell and inhabit, individually and communally. Bogart asks the important question, "What is the story I/we wish to tell?"

So I'm asking you right now: what is your story? Your genuine story. How do you want to tell it? What does telling your story teach you about yourself?

Perhaps the most powerful stories are those we tell ourselves. We may tell ourselves that we have no power, or that power is innately bad. Then what? That leaves all the action to those who are comfortable with power, oftentimes those who claim that privilege by virtue of wealth, race, gender, or other cultural demographics, and then often abuse that privilege. When we begin to tell ourselves that we too have the ability to act, and that this power grows when we discover, develop, and share it in solidarity with like-minded humans, things change. Things break open.

As an opera singer, I'm often asked about the stereotype of a woman's voice breaking a glass. Sorry if it disappoints you, but I've never sung near a wine glass thin enough to break with the vibrations of my voice. However, once while I was singing a high C in a hotel ballroom, the huge, glass windows behind the audience began vibrating sympathetically, emitting another C, two octaves below the note I sang. That was a powerful moment.

So, go on, tell me: what's your superpower? How does it feel and how will you use it?

The body of the genuine

The physical phenomenon of our voice constitutes a unique aspect of our personhood, a calling card if you will. This encompasses not only your physical sound–high or low timbre, and your unique resonance, smooth or scratchy, booming or tender–a result of your physiology, the shape of the bones in your face and ribcage, the size of your larynx and vocal cords, as well as the way you've been taught and conditioned to use them.

Your voice also includes the way you express yourself in words, in music, in visual art, in any medium of your choosing. Your voice can carry the sound, style, and expression most natural, most organic, and most beneficial to you. No two voices are alike: a fact used in some instances as a recognition device. Even if someone imitates you, your voice will still ring as unique. Remember in the animated movie *Happy Feet* when the baby penguins find their mothers by the sounds of their songs? There's a human truth in that too.

Vocation – your life speaks

When we tell the story of our career, what we do in life, we might choose the word "vocation." This term relates to the notion of "calling," often reserved for what may be considered "noble" professions, such as doctors, teachers, faith leaders, artists. Parker Palmer, the renowned teacher of teachers and guide for "Courageous Living"[1], explores how the word "vocation" derives from the Latin root for voice–*vox, voce, vocale.* And this applies not only to

---

1. Center for Courage & Renewal

certain occupations or disciplines (like voice), but rather to one's deeper response to that which you feel a call, a mission, a reason for your work, your being, your life. What voice calls to you? Can you make the time and space to listen deeply to it?

In his small and powerful book, *Let your Life Speak,* Palmer urges us "to sense that, running beneath the surface of the experience I call life, there is a deeper and truer life waiting to be acknowledged".[2] He quotes the poetry of lesbian writer May Sarton and her "quest for vocation":

Now I become myself.
It's taken time, many years and places.
I have been dissolved and shaken,
Worn other people's faces . . .

Vocation of course pertains to much, much more than any kind of career or service profession. We all have at least one, often more than one, calling in our lifetimes; a voice that beckons us to serve and interact with the world in a particular field. Perhaps you are a teacher; you may be a writer, or sheep herder, a butcher baker or candlestick maker. Maybe, like me during Ari's preschool years, your calling is to raise wonderful humans, or to create a gracious home and garden. Or, just maybe, like so many in our country, you are working several minimum wage jobs to feed yourself and your family.

All of this is potentially noble, because vocation refers not just to what you do but *how you do it*. If you feel that sense of rightness in your profession, in how you show up in the world, if you are "all in" with the doing of it, then you are responding to a call. You are living out your vocation.

Where does this voice, this call, come from? Is it from a divine

---

2. Palmer, Parker, *Let your Life Speak,* pg. 5

and mysterious source, or from within yourself? I wonder, how much of it includes a prescribed list of qualities required by a colonizing institution or capitalist system? Take a moment to stop and think about the times you've heard or felt a calling to something, somewhere.

Theologian and spiritual writer Frederick Buechner, in his book *Wishful Thinking: A Seeker's ABC*, somewhat famously said, "The place God calls you to is the place where your deep gladness and the world's deep hunger meet." You do not have to regard G*d with any specific name for this to hold true: whether you believe in Allah, Jesus, Buddha, Higher Power, or just the mystery and beauty of creation, whatever calls you from deep inside and far beyond, that's the voice Boechner speaks of. To hear that voice, it helps to quiet all the other voices in our heads, on our shoulders, and in the media.

To be honest, I'm not quite sure whether I agree with Buechner on the "world's hunger" part. If you are at all like me, the needs of others make up a cacophony of loud voices whose demands can immobilize your authentic life. You may feel called to write, and your family needs you to make dinner. You feel called to paint, and your landlord needs you to make a better living and pay the rent. What if you hear a calling toward a vocation for which you don't yet perceive a hunger in the world, maybe a vocation that doesn't even exist yet. Should you stop and ignore the call? I don't think so. Please don't stop.

Howard Thurman, whose quote about the "sound of the genuine" began this movement, says this (if you've received an email from me, you've read it in my signature block): "Don't ask what the world needs. Ask what makes you come alive and go do it. Because what the world needs is people who have come alive".[3] That makes sense to me. Let's come alive first.

Ultimately, it may come down to trust: in a higher power, in the world, in yourself. In a culture where, especially as women and others with marginalized voices, we are most often told not to trust our instincts, to go with our gut can feel like an act of rebellion. Yet, how many times have you second-guessed yourself, only later to regret not making your instinctive choice?

Fun fact: the word "confidence" derives from two Latin words–*con,* meaning with, and *fidentem,* meaning trust and belief. That's right, confidence–in yourself, in others–begins with developing an unshakable belief and trust. If we are about building our confidence, we might want to take a look at our level of trust. That, friends, might just take us to the area of spirit and faith. Buckle up.

Your Spiritual Voice

Now, don't get nervous. I'm not going to try and force a belief system on you. Quite the contrary. As someone who spent years of my life welcoming humans on the margins–women, BIPOC, queer, trans, disabled–into the communities of faith that I was privileged to lead, only to have that faith tradition or community ultimately hurt or reject them, I'd like something much more life-giving for you. I'd like you to hear and follow your true spiritual calling.

Perhaps that means learning more about the spiritual traditions of your ancestors. Maybe it means creating a faith practice that brings you closer to the natural world. My own cultural path as both a child of the Pacific Northwest and a descendent of Celtic ancestors brought me to Celtic spirituality.

---

3. A verbal statement from Thurman, quoted by Gil Bailie, in a book section titled "In Gratitude".

In his book, *Listening for the Heartbeat of God,* J. Philip Newell describes this "stream of Celtic spirituality" as "characterized by the expectation of finding God within, of hearing the living voice of God speaking from the very heart of life, within creation and within ourselves." As one who deeply values spiritual mysticism, rather than colonizing doctrines, my heart finds its home in "a spirituality that sees God in the whole of life and regards all things as inter-related."[4]

Your heart may lead you to explore many wisdom traditions until you find your place of the genuine, the place where you feel seen and challenged as your true self. This journey may, as mine did, lead you more deeply into the traditions of your cultural ancestors. You may find yourself challenged and transformed; you will probably cry, and that's ok. And. Wherever Spirit leads you, there is some baggage I lovingly suggest you leave at the door:

Shame. A byproduct of the binary and misogynistic system of the ancient Greeks and Romans that still undergirds society–honor and shame–shame has no place in an enlightened spiritual experience. Shame may seek you through the values and theology of a tradition, in the voices of family members, or, heaven forbid, the voices of those in power. When it does, simply refuse. Hard pass. I like to declare the space I'm in as a "no shame zone" and I invite you to do the same.

Certainty. When you meet someone who says they have all the answers, run. Spirit is a mystery to explore, not just a bunch of immovable rules to follow. Question everything. It might make others uncomfortable, which provides them with an opportunity for growth. If you find yourself in an environment where the goal is other than to wonder and grow, you are free to walk away. Really. Buh bye.

Here's the most important piece of wisdom I've gained in my

---

4. Newell, J. Philip, *Listening for the Heartbeat of God,* pgs. 94-97

lifetime of spiritual seeking and decades of study and leadership: you are loved. You are loved. Period. Especially if you find yourself on the margins; that's just where my example, Jesus of Nazareth, did some of his best work. You deserve inclusion, belonging, and justice. I'd love to talk to you more about it, one on one.

For now, here's an exercise to try:

Wherever you are right now—sitting in a comfy chair, relaxing on the beach, feeling the sun on your face or the wind in your hair, or even (especially?) in front of your messy desk with a load of dishes waiting in the sink—I want you to let go. No, really! Just allow that chair, the floor, or the sand to fully support you. Remind yourself that you are safe, that the universe is a friendly place, by and large, and that you have people and energies that support you fully.

Now, listen. Listen to the beating of your own heart. Listen to the voice within that is uniquely yours. What is it telling you? I hope it's saying something like: "You are sufficient. You are not too much, or too little. You are safe to explore." If you can't hear it yet, hear me saying it, or hear a dear friend or mentor, because it is true. Oh, my dear one, it is so very, very true.

Write about it for a moment. You've got time. You're worth it.

I'll wait.

Above the Madding Crowd

As Thurman observed, sometimes (often) we cannot hear the voice of our calling above the noise of the other "helpful voices" in our heads. Time and again, as we mature and become truer to ourselves, we need support to differentiate who we *are* from who we think we *should be*. Here's an imaginative exercise that has helped me and my clients:

Imagine being in a car, filled with all the many voices in your life–your mother, perhaps criticizing your driving or your outfit; your father telling you to slow down and be careful that you don't get hurt or look silly; your second grade teacher telling you that you cannot spell or that your penhumanship is sloppy; your ex-partner telling you that you are too fat; your grandmother complaining that you don't eat enough; a high-powered executive telling you to reach your potential; and a stay-at-home parent telling you to spend more time with family. Imagine pulling over (safely), slamming on the breaks and shouting, "ENOUGH!"

In a calmer voice (or not), you may say something to those voices like, "I appreciate that you've all done your best to keep me safe these many years. Thank you. And I'm an adult now. I no longer need your protection. You can stay in the car if you want to, but you have to quiet down the advice, and you are definitely not doing any driving!"

Now, listen to the quiet, the vibrating softness of air that has yet to be filled with sound. From that place, what do you hear next?

What do you feel, see, smell, taste? What is your own inner wisdom telling you?

That inner voice, perhaps timid at first and then growing stronger with use, sounds a bit like, well, YOU! Its tones fill you with peace and joy, and the more deeply you listen, the more you know which way to go. You may not have all the directions, and can certainly ask for help on your terms; you may even need to fill up your tank to get there. For now, I invite you to just step on the gas and head on out.

To help underscore this lesson, I'd like to share a story from one of my former clients and current friends (with her full permission and participation). This will be the first of several such stories throughout the book, and each story-sharer partners with me in the success of our book.

Clara's story: Artist at the Wheel

On the hour-long drive between my family's farm and the nearest town forty miles away, my mom would drive, my sister would sit up front, and I would sit in the back. I often got tension headaches as a kid. Later in life I would think a lot about what caused them, but at the time my parents believed they were triggered by excitement or overstimulation, such as the eagerly awaited weekly shopping trip. Too frequently on the drive home I would be lying down in the back seat, sick with a pounding headache.

When I wasn't sick, I also liked to lie down in the back seat and be in my own world. I'd ask my mom to play some of my favorite classical tape cassettes. Debussy's "La Mer." Saint-Saëns' "Carnival of the Animals." With the music turned up and my eyes focused on the landscape moving past our car windows I would have a kind of private sublime experience. Watching the cottonwood trees in the evening summer light against the mountains. Or in the winter, watching the moon flashing across frozen river flats. I felt a relationship with the music that was emotional and purely my own.

My family was immersed in the all-consuming daily life of caring for animals, vegetable gardens, and managing the many challenges of living in rural Alaska, a region inundated with snow and freezing temperatures for most of the year. Internally, alongside this intense relationship with nature and homesteading, I somehow knew that I was an artist. That making art, whether drawing in my room or secretly singing while I fed the farm animals, was my way of cultivating an inner self, separate from my family, while also connecting with a world beyond our own.

I was a teenager when Joyce toured her opera company to my hometown's performing arts center–a production of Madame Butterfly. *Joyce offered a singing workshop, and I had the opportunity to talk with her and take the class. I was very nervous and shy, but I knew I wanted to study with her. I wanted to connect with her ability to create a sound so shimmering and ethereal, yet powerful. More powerful than one could imagine an unamplified voice could be. The artform gave me shivers. Opera connected me with something bigger...the past and places far away, while also requiring a very present awareness and focus.*

When I went to college, I became Joyce's student and worked with her company in a number of ways. Singing led to performing, designing, and assisting on productions. Later in other cities I acted in plays, started coaching acting for singers, assisting directors, and directing. Now, alongside curating art exhibitions with my husband, I organize concerts and host composers and performers for film shoots and short stays on the farm where we live outside of Philadelphia. I devote a large portion of my days to gardening, growing flowers, and am a floral designer. Singing didn't become the thing. It was a pathway to a multitude of things. My early years with Joyce helped me develop confidence to follow the artist's path, and exploring characters and narratives in performance showed me experientially that there are myriad ways of being. Somehow, I knew as a small child that I needed this container called "art," something bigger than myself, to help me understand and create meaning in my life.

Still, for a long time, driving terrified me. When I left home, I lived without a car in different towns and cities. Some had good public transit, some had little to none. I told myself I couldn't afford a car, which on a limited income was true, but it was really more because I felt incapable of driving. I modified my life—where I lived, worked, and all my relationships and activities—around my ability to walk, take a bus, or catch a ride to wherever I needed to go. In my 30s I moved to semi-rural/suburban Bucks County, Pennsylvania to be with my future husband. Thrown into a labyrinth of towns connected by fast, winding roads with no public transit, I finally realized the severity of my driving phobia. It took several years, with the help of a therapist and my partner, to get me on the road. While I still have my limits and often feel like an imposter behind the wheel, I commute regularly to work and can run all the errands necessary to our daily lives. The more I realized how I had distilled long-held anxieties into a kind of self-generated disability—being unable to drive—the more I also began to realize how my life in the arts had acted as a bridge. It showed me a way forward that was, in its ideal expression, focused on connection, communication, collaboration, and kindness. In creating, I felt possibility.

Now when I drive our car to work, I listen to my favorite local classical radio station. Recently they played a piece of lieder by Schubert as I was passing the horse fields on my way home. I was struck by the thought, "This is for me." Not in a possessive way, but really "this is for me." In Thich Nhat Hanh's books he writes about the need to be present for things to be able to appreciate them. To the moon, we can say "I am here for you" and appreciate it more fully. To our loved ones, "Darling, I am here for you." This allows us to find a way in, into a deeper relationship or experience of the moon or our loved ones. There is something about an early relationship with music and our creative voice that runs very deep. It is not theoretical, or beyond reach. It's very personal. It's here for us.

Do I contradict myself?
Very well then, I contradict myself,
(I am large, I contain multitudes.)

— Walt Whitman, *Song of Myself*

Explore Those Multitudes

Clara's story depicts how your creative voice can express itself in a variety of ways: music, gardening, theatre, poetry. While you're on this journey toward fullness, I invite you to venture into many different mediums. Allow yourself to expand and explore and notice the power of your voice as you practice these activities.

While you do so, I invite you to resist the urge to narrow your choices right out of the gate. This tendency comes, at least in part, from the influence of our capitalist society, insisting that we specialize and market ourselves in one profitable field of experience. Instead, be like Whitman–be large. Allow your path to take you in various directions, and for those mediums, those experiences, to inform one another.

Here are just some of the many paths to explore:

Visual art

Despite what you may have been told and may now tell yourself, visual art, whether with paint or pencil or pastels, is not the sole province of professional artists. For an excellent book on this notion, read (or re-read) *The Artist's Way* by Julia Cameron. In some cases, choosing an unfamiliar medium like visual art may help lead you in an important direction.

During my journey through chemotherapy for early-stage breast cancer, words abandoned me. As chemicals flooded my body and brain, written and spoken language seemed to float away like flotsam from a shipwreck. Yet there was so much I had to express, process, get outside of my inner experience. So I went to friend and painter, Jim Fowler, and asked him to teach me about painting as a medium.

Jim kindly opened the way to using paint, color, and texture as gracious tools to help me describe my inner experience. He introduced me to a substance called gesso, that slows down the drying process of acrylic paint and lets you build up a thicker texture, similar to (but less expensive and toxic than) oil paints; he gave me heavy watercolor paper to stand in for intimidating canvases. Jim gave me permission to let go of the subjective judgements of whether a creation was "good" and encouraged me to focus only on what felt true.

For months, whenever my emotions spilled over, I brushed them onto surfaces with color, texture, and gesture; roiling seas, bridges to nowhere, and scorching deserts all depicted an internal landscape I could not describe in words. It helped.

Painting is what appealed to me, having experienced it through my father, my brother, and my painterly friends. For you the medium may be drawing, weaving, knitting, or working with glass or clay. Dig deep and listen to the visual art mediums that beckon you and follow them.

You may also choose to find a trustworthy teacher or mentor. Ask them to meet you where you are. Trust the process and shut off that inner, critical voice. Practice. Stretch your creating muscles, trust your instinct. Do not try to be anyone else or tell anyone else's story–or, perhaps worse, someone else's version of your story. If you'd like to speak with me about partnering with you on this sacred quest, I'm here for that.

Filling the Room may inspire you to fill your hands, fill the paper, fill the canvas or the kiln. The soul of your eyes may reveal to you and the world an inner truth that surprises you and challenges others. When that happens, breathe and flow. Breathe and flow.

Movement

I avoid using the word "dance" when encouraging people to try this form of expression. "Dance" often brings up intimidating images of pointe shoes and thin legs or complicated routines with hats and canes. If this is just up your alley–good for you! Dance away! If not, don't allow this to close the door on expressing your story with your body.

Movement, one of our most primal forms of expression, is available to all of us from the time we are very young. Can you recall a time when you, as a youngster, moved unselfconsciously to music? Take a moment to remember and record some details.

For me, it was the sunny afternoon in my childhood when my grandmother–tiny Evelyn, nicknamed "Mug," standing barely five feet–tried to teach me to do the twist in our suburban backyard. I can still see the unbridled joy in our faces and hear our laughter when we eventually fell into the grass together. If you close your eyes, can you see and feel the joy in the heart of your younger, less inhibited self? Now, see if you can channel that joy into your arm, your hand, your foot. What does your body want to do, if you'll let it? Go ahead–no one's watching.

Our bodies remember things that our minds cannot or may choose not to. Joyful things, and sometimes sad things, difficult things. To keep us whole and safe in times of trauma, our body stores parts of those memories away from our consciousness, where it waits for a time when we may be ready to reintegrate that memory into our story.

I began seminary roughly a year after my cancer treatments were completed. Great idea, huh? Because I was fine, *right?* Excited to have cheated death, I felt ready and eager for learning new things and moving the hell on. In retrospect, I behaved rather like Ebenezer Scrooge when he woke up and found out he hadn't missed Christmas: determined to get going and do great things, and maybe seeming a little bit unhinged. But, as Bessel Van Der Kolk revealed in his seminal work *The Body Keeps the Score*, my body remembered.

Blessedly, in my Sacred Dance for Healing class at the Pacific School of Religion in Berkeley, California, taught by the mother of liturgical movement, Carla De Sola, we listened to our bodies. Carla's class, with its focus on the spiritual and healing knowledge hidden in our bodies, revealed to me the pain that still lived (rent free) inside my multitudinous self, needing awareness and healing.

One day, as I lay on the cold, wooden floor during an opening movement meditation, my body felt safe enough to remember all the cold, hard tables upon which I'd lain in the past two years of treatment and tests. Eyes closed, I curled up like a baby and wept the forgotten tears impeding my healing and growth. The tears formed a great river, one that swept me down, through my pristine, Episcopal, English garden, through the messy, primordial mud, and into the roots of the Tree of Life. This moment of profound, fruitful realization blossomed into a new path of creativity, integrated with spirituality and healing for me—one that led to new compositions, new ministries, and new adventures. It led me to this voice, this book, and to you. You just never know.

Whether you choose to move on your own in a meditative or ecstatic dance, or to join a group in improvised and/or choreographed movement, remember you're still the one driving your own car. Put those critical voices in the back seat, or on the side of the road if necessary. This is your story. Your voice. Your body. Your memory.

Writing

By the time I finished grad school, I thought I never wanted to write again. Academic writing, with its strict forms and rules, most of them devised by patriarchal hierarchy, was never really my favorite jam. And it took me so long to conform to this discipline, I worried that my creativity might never return. Luckily, poetry exists.

As a white, straight, cisgendered woman, even as a counselor, an artist, and a feminist, I've been profoundly impacted by the hierarchy of modes of expression in society. Words, words, and words, strung together in a linear format (complete with the correct annotations), within the constraints of dominant culture logic, tend to receive more attention and notoriety. More money as well. What could be more synonymous with obscure poverty than the voice of a poet? And who could better reimagine revolutionary forms of expression?

As the voices of 20th and 21st century women poets like Emily Dickinson, Maya Angelou, Mary Oliver, and recent youth poet laureate Amanda Gorman captured public imagination, other forms of storytelling have come into the light. In her poem *The Hill We Climb,* that she spoke at the inauguration of President Joe Biden, Gorman proclaimed:

When day comes we ask ourselves,
where can we find light in this never-ending shade?
The loss we carry,
a sea we must wade
We've braved the belly of the beast
We've learned that quiet isn't always peace
And the norms and notions
of what just is
Isn't always just-ice . . .

Modern and post-modern poetry, written with new patterns of meter and rhyme, begins to break open form and genre, even words themselves, in ways that I find liberating. Poet e.e. cummings stretched the boundaries of punctuation, and coined new words like "puddlewonderful" and "watersmooth." There is something holy about the kind of creative honesty available in poetry.

When doing research for my dissertation among women surviving breast cancer, I asked women about texts they considered sacred and helpful to their healing. Among the most frequently cited texts were poems by Mary Oliver.

After years of reading and hearing it, my heart still cracks open afresh at her poem "Wild Geese." In the recent movie telling the story of marathon swimmer Diane Nyad, a single phrase from Oliver's poem, "A Summer's Day," even though often quoted, turned things around for Nyad and her best friend, Bonnie, when it challenged them: "What is it you will do with your one wild and precious life?" To quote actor Sandra Oh addressing audiences of Shakespeare during these uncertain times: "What you will. *What will you?*"

Now, you don't have to be an award-winning poet, or a poet at all, to use words as your medium of expression. Essays, short stories, novels, and creative nonfiction can all tell part of your story and make connections between lives. Perhaps there are stories and forms from your culture of ancestry–folk tales, Indigenous wisdom, Celtic stories. Incorporating and studying these stories may help you find and strengthen your unique voice.

Consider reading groundbreaking texts by professor bell hooks, especially *Teaching to Transgress,* wherein they explore "Language: Teaching New Worlds/New Words" asserting, "Like desire, language disrupts, refuses to be contained within boundaries." hooks quotes a line from queer black poet Adrienne Rich's poem "The Burning of Paper Instead of Children" that has "moved and disturbed something within" (them):

an age of long silence

relief

from this tongue this slab of limestone
or reinforced concrete
fanatics and traders
dumped on this coast wildgreen clayred
that breathed once
in signals of smoke
sweep of the wind

knowledge of the oppressor
this is the oppressor's language

yet I need it to talk to you[5]

Talk to me.

---

5. hooks, bell, *Teaching to Transgress,* pg. 167

Room for Silence

"In order to see birds it is necessary to become part of the silence."

— Robert Lynd, Irish poet and activist

A word about silence.

Silence speaks too. It can certainly fill a room, a cathedral, a forest. There are different qualities of silence: silence that sits; silence that yearns; silence that challenges.

As an extrovert, I struggle with silence sometimes. Still an occasional "fixer" thanks to my past of trauma and hypervigilance, silence both kept me safe and placed me in danger. My internal argument ensues: "On the one hand, what if no one says anything? How will we make things better? On the other hand, who says I am the one to break that silence?" Blessedly, over the years, I've learned to welcome silence, as it can do a great deal of emotional lifting. I've given it qualified trust, and great things often happen!

When I sit to meditate, at first, a waterfall of thought flows down through my mind, begging to be noticed and spoken. After some practice, it slows to an easy trickle of noticing: "oh, there's that thought! And there's that emotion again!"

Nature inhabits silence the most gracefully, I think, or at least what passes for silence to us humans. My counselor in Alaska once directed me outdoors for deep insight.

"See those mountains?" she asked. "What do you think when you look at them? Do you say 'How dare they? Who do they think they are, standing so tall and proud?'"

I remember laughing, "No, of course not! I see in them the beauty of Creation. They inspire me to do more."

She smiled, and said, "Exactly. When you stand on the stage, full of beautiful music, your strength and life force inspire others beyond what they may think possible."

And so it was that I came to think of even my silences in a concert, waiting for my entrances, listening to the choir and the orchestra, as a kind of prayer, a blessing, an incantation. The silence of a presiding priestess.

How, then, can I write silence into this book, too? With an invitation.

Close these pages when you reach the end of this section.

Yup, close them (mark them with your cool new Fill the Room bookmark and return later). Then, step outdoors, wherever you are. Let the free air fill you with its light and life. Breathe out your gratitude for all that is in and around you. Notice. The sunlight, breaking through the clouds, like an idea, a welcoming smile. The rain and mist gently nourishing the earth. If you're surrounded by buildings, that's ok; if you can get out of town, that's even better.

Feel your spine stretch like the tall trunk of a lodgepole pine; if your spine doesn't stretch like that, stretch out your spirit. Reach out your arms and imagination like the limbs of a sacred cedar, beyond your fingertips, touching the energy of the trees around you, however far away.

Now, open the crown of your head to the wisdom of the Universe, of G*d as you understand them, your ancestors, or just the goodness of life itself. Open the eyes and ears of *your heart to receive the messages, blessings and inspiration of leaf rustle, squirrel chatter, bird call, child's laughter. In the silence. Take up your space in the symphonic score of life.*

Trust.

Your Big, Loud, Scary Voice

Does your own voice ever scare you? What have you learned about the danger of speaking up and out? Have you ever been accused by a dominant voice of being selfish? Was there a punishment for that? Then consider: is it just possible that the goal of being selfless belongs to the dominant, foisted upon those on the margins to keep us quiet and maintain the status quo? If so, might resistance also be possible?

My voice has always been pleasant, moving, even beautiful, some might say. In fact, a theater director friend of mine suggested I record the sounds of my labor with Ariana, certain that I would emit soaring, inspiring tones. In actuality, the final words I uttered–screamed more like it–before my baby finally shot out of my koochie were "GET OUT!!" in a tone that stunned my other children into lasting respect and a temporary fear of procreation.

This voice–something my husband calls my "weirding voice", after the Bene Gesserit nuns in the science fiction story of *Dune*– rarely makes an appearance in my life, but when it does, boy howdy, people listen. It astonishes even me, as it seems to rise out of a deep, hidden part of myself that I seldom access, carrying intentions which lay dormant for long periods of time.

Some of us grew up with families of origin where angry voices ruled the day. I learned to adjust my responses to any conflict and be on the lookout for a potential outburst from another family member, which I then felt responsible to manage. Therefore, my big, loud voice had to be reserved for special, safe places. Strangely, for me that was the opera stage. For much of my life, the safest place for me to express myself was in front of hundreds of people, not one-on-one.

How about you? Do you get to use your big, loud voice? Where, when, and how? When you do, does it scare you? Excite you? Embarrass you? Whatever way it makes you feel, I'm here to tell you this truth: that big, loud, scary voice which is a part of you is not ugly. It's as beautiful as all the parts of large, diverse, multitudinous you!

You can choose where to use it: maybe singing, acting, or protesting, or in a room full of things you pay money to break. I've witnessed people using it on karaoke night surrounded by friends and/or total strangers. You can also find a mental health provider who can give you permission, if needed, and tools for befriending and using your "weirding voice" along your journey of self-discovery.

Journeys

Sometimes, you must begin your journey before you fully understand its purpose. Ancient monks went on pilgrimages that they called *peregrinatio*, which means "to wander." They got in a small boat, without even an oar or rudder, and simply let the current take them where it would. Now, that sounds terrifying to me, but it worked out well for saints like Columbinus, who washed up on the shores of an island in the Outer Hebrides off the coast of Scotland, called Iona. There St. Columba founded a monastery that became one of the centers of Celtic spirituality to this day. All that from simply wandering.

A note about the term "pilgrim." While the term may conjure images of uptight religious people wearing black clothing with big white collars and buckles on their shoes (there to colonize indigenous folx and get rewarded with a holiday), the term *pilgrim* has a much deeper and broader meaning. Throughout history, "pilgrim" meant anyone on a journey of discovery, generally in a place foreign to them. Most often, these journeys were spiritual in nature, and they were practiced in a variety of religious traditions.

For example, the Hajj refers to an annual pilgrimage taken to the holy city of Mecca in Saudi Arabia, a practice required of all able, adult Muslims at least once in their lifetimes. One of the Five Pillars of Islam, this tradition dates back all the way to the time of the prophet Abraham.

Even in ways not always overtly religious or spiritual, people still travel to learn more about themselves. My husband, Patrick, a teacher and actor who moved to the Alaskan tundra to teach school there, says that he learned most about his own identity when amid an unfamiliar culture and landscape. We travel to discover, or we read books, attend the theatre, and listen to podcasts. A pilgrimage invites us into what can be called a liminal or "in between" space. You may have heard the term "thin place," where the temporal and spiritual worlds come close together. These are places where we meet our deepest selves and encounter the holy. The best journeys, of course, require some messiness, humility and discomfort.

While on my own sabbatical pilgrimage to the British Isles (funded by a renewal grant from the Lilly Endowment), I meticulously planned most of the three-month trip, and I intentionally left a piece of the journey open to the currents. I longed to visit the west coast of Ireland, particularly the wilds of Connemara, but didn't know how I would get there.

Poet John O'Donohue lived there, and wrote passionately about this beautiful and unique landscape, full of grasses and bogs, ocean and stones, and I longed to see it with my own eyes. In O'Donohue's own words, etched onto his gravestone overlooking the sea in the Burren of County Clare:

May I have the courage today
To live the life that I would love
To postpone my dream no longer
But do at least what I came here for
And waste my heart on fear no more.

While waiting in Dublin for my path to Connemara to open up to me, out of the blue (well, out of social media, really) I received a message from the midwife who helped me birth Ari in Alaska decades ago. Kaye had been following me on Facebook, and as luck would have it, she currently lived in Ireland with her own adult daughter and grandkids. She'd read about my journey, and wanted to travel with me to Galway and beyond; would I like a ride?

Thus began a chapter of my sabbatical full of deep wisdom, memories, and healed wounds. As we drove and hiked through this inspiring landscape, we shared so many stories of our times living and leading in Southeast Alaska. Stories about dashed hopes, betrayals, as well as amazing successes and dreams fulfilled. For each of us, hearing the other's stories was both surprising and comforting. In those hills, the Creator's voice cried out to me, "Why would I create you with so much beauty, so much passion, with such a voice, for you to simply throw it away? I would never require such a stupid sacrifice; I rejoice in your living fully!"

After three months of listening to the landscapes of Ireland, Scotland and my ancestors' land of Wales, the message truly sank in. I would return home and resign from my death-dealing job serving an institution that neither saw nor valued me or other marginalized or innovative voices. I would spend the next six months wandering the land of my own curiosity, on a pilgrimage of discernment to find the place where my life, my heart, and my vocation could come together. Journeys can beget other journeys.

The following summer, when the COVID pandemic had

eased substantially, I returned to Scotland to premiere a piece of vocal performance at the Fringe Festival in Edinburgh. With Ari directing, we performed at long last a piece composed with me by Stefan Hakenberg, based on images from Carla's class, and my time in the breast MRI machine. Such a wild ride, complete with busking in the street, reuniting with colleagues from around the world, and best of all meeting and thrilling at the talents of brave, innovative performers.

While in Edinburgh, we experienced the great honor of hearing and meeting poet, comic, and gender nonbinary prophet Alok Vaid-Menon. In a small, black box space outside the central festival, they blew our minds and hearts wide open with statements like:

> We want a world where boys can feel, girls can lead, and the rest of us can not only exist but thrive. This is not about erasing men and women but rather acknowledging that man and woman are two of many stars in a constellation that do not compete but amplify one another's shine.

What about you? What journey calls to your wild heart? Which seeming detours frighten you? What would happen if you embraced them? With whom might you connect on your journey of discovery?

You've made new steps in rediscovering your true voice. I hope and trust that these discoveries will continue to unfold for you for as long as you draw breath. You'll undoubtedly find new paths to discovery, and I invite you to share them with me, with us.

For now, in the next movement, let's turn to developing your powerful voice. This may begin with some healing, and with building your courage to speak your truth, your narrative, your dreams for this world. You can do it, one breath at a time.

I'm here with you. Let's go!

Second Movement: Develop

One voice can change a room, and if one voice can change a room, then it can change a city, and if it can change a city, it can change a state, and if it can change a state, it can change a nation, and if it can change a nation, it can change the world.

— *Barack Obama*

The only thing better than singing is more singing.

— *Ella Fitzgerald*

Libera Me

WHAT WAS I THINKING? WHY AM I DOING THIS TO MYSELF?

My heart hammers as I rise slowly from my chair, numb underarm crammed into my black taffeta gown. Smiling serenely, continuing my calm breathing–in and out, in and out–for a terrifying moment I behold what I am about to do. Launch into the

55

soprano solo in Verdi's *Requiem*, one of the most difficult and dramatic vocal pieces ever written—a week after I started chemotherapy, and two days after completely losing my voice.

For years I'd dreamed of soloing in *Requiem*, a sacred oratorio composed for a 100-voice choir, 100-piece symphony orchestra, and a quartet of soloists. Now here I stand, beaming my radiant energy into the room, while feeling as though I'm stark naked. There is no character to shield me, as in the Verdi operas I'd sung previously. No giddy Violetta, no forthright Mistress Ford to protect me. Only chanting desperate prayers for peace and freedom at the end of life, staring death in the eye, in front of a thousand people. It's too late to turn back now.

In studying for the performance, I learned that Verdi had composed this sweeping, fifteen-movement piece backward: he began at the end, with the soprano aria, found his theme, and worked his way back from there. This solo—this moment—contained everything, and I feel everything fill me right now. What was that song by Lauren Hill? *Everything is everything. What is meant to be will be...Change, it comes eventually...* In this moment, all of my experiences, my hard work, my triumphs, my disasters, all of it meets right here and now.

Breathing fully, I open my mouth and intone the first words on a single note, an A flat, in the center of my range, the center of my being, but hurriedly, with desperation and passion:

Libera me, Dómine, de morte ætérna In die illa treménda
(Free me, o God, from eternal death in this day of your tremendous judgment)

Freedom, yes. I long to be freed from the medical ordeal that stretches before me; and I welcome the freedom that comes with accepting my mortality, and at the same time freeing myself from

56

limitations. Doing something so hard right now with so little in reserve. Free me; help me.

To illustrate the word *tremenda*, Verdi introduces the strings with a trembling minor chord. My voice soars up to summon the heavens (*coeli*), then plummets into my chest voice for the phrase's earthly conclusion (*terra*):

Quando cœli movéndi sunt et terra!
(When the heavens and earth are moved!)

The chorus enters after my opening statement, almost chanting, echoing my words in a calmer tone **Libera me, Dómine, de morte ætérna.** They are my friends and neighbors, including some of my students. We've rehearsed together for weeks, past my initial diagnosis and surgery, and into treatments. Many of them know what's at stake here. For all of us. And we're here for it.

Patrick sits somewhere in the auditorium, his muscles tense, taking every breath along with me. Pat's been there every step of this journey to the underworld—holding my hair back when I vomited and holding my body as my hair began to fall out.

He was beside me two days earlier, when ferocious chemo-induced gastric reflux wiped out my voice overnight. Nothing was left, only a little squeak. He drove me to my primary care doctor, where I received strong steroids to take down the swelling and a hug for luck. Pat held my hand as I rested and miraculously recovered, and now he, too, prayed for strength and freedom. Phrase by phrase, breath by breath...

BAM! With one note from the foreboding bassoon, Verdi grabs us and sends us off on another wild phrase, driven by undulating strings:

Dum veneris judicare saeculum per ignem!
When you will come to judge the age with fire!

The woodwinds follow tentatively, trying to get us under control. But it's no use: we cannot contain the stream of anxiety bubbling up. My voice pleads once again in my lowest register, punctuated by explosive consonants, popping like cuss words off my teeth.

> **Tremens Factus sum ego, et timeo, dum**
> **Discussio venerit, atque ventura ira.**
> **I tremble, and I am afraid, since trial and**
> **anger are coming.**

It feels so right to sing like that, to release the anger and terror running beneath my tranquil exterior. Like Janis Joplin, or the Smashing Pumpkins, snarling and screaming my head off in the face of this lousy disease. Come on! Come on and take it!

Then a short reprieve, as the orchestra and chorus take up my theme, with brass and timpani pounding away, reverberating in our bones. Although they're singing the Latin verses of the funeral Mass, in my heart I hear them instead saying, "Fuck this! Fuck this! Fuck this shit!" One body, one intention, many voices singing bravely into a storm of wrath.

> **Dies illa, dies irae, calamitatis et miseriae,**
> **Dies illa, dies magna et amara valde.**
> **That day, a day of anger, disaster and sorrow, a**
> **mighty day, and exceedingly bitter.**

During a lull, before the woodwinds summon my next, gentler phrase with a series of F sharps, I glance briefly at my quartet colleagues: baritone, tenor and mezzo. None of them know about my situation; I didn't want them to pity me or take it easy with our work. If I can share in their oblivion, I thought, and pretend that I am well, that this is easy, then it might become true. Maybe. After *all, I've done hard things before–giving birth, twice, moving across country. Twice.*

At least the strap of my gown on the surgery side is staying up thanks to a piece of double-stick tape from Beth, the red-haired mezzo. Our two women's voices, with different and unique timbres, combine into a strong and organic third sound. We feel like sisters, and as I notice the upturned corners of her mouth, I know what she's thinking: "Rock it, girl!" I breathe, trill my rr's and float above the chorus:

> **Requiem, requiem aeternam dona eis, Domine,**
> **et lux perpetua luceat eis.**
> **Give them eternal rest, Lord, and may light**
> **perpetual shine upon them.**

Give us peace, please, please. Tears spring to my eyes and I let them fall, hoping they don't choke me with snot. As I approach the upcoming high note, I can feel us all holding our breath, praying. I imagine Marianne, my voice teacher of many years and herself a cancer survivor, pushing her little hand into my abdomen.

"Hook it, right here!" she would insist, with an intensity that is both motivating and a little scary.

Marianne survived so much–Nazi Germany, the deaths of both her children. She understood how to channel grief into work. I can feel her standing beside me now, all five feet of her. As the chorus weaves a cushion of sound beneath me, I spin the word "Requiem" on a high B natural, a pinpoint of light to pierce the darkness. Peace.

But it's not over, not hardly. Now we head into the final stretch, "Libera Me!" we demand–singers, percussion, brass, all of us–as the conductor urges us ahead with his baton, and the audience perches on the edge of their seats. Together, we overcome our fears. The vibrations of each instrument propel us forward like a fiery wind toward the climax.

I dare and take flight. I sing with more abandon, more power, and more beauty than ever before or since. My feet grounded into the earth, my head open to the heavens, my voice catapults up to a high C, above the entire orchestra and chorus, before descending into my chest voice for the final, chanted statement.

Libera me. Libera me. Libera me.

As the final notes dissipate, I briefly think, "hot damn!" I did it. My voice didn't crack or falter.

I am free. At least for now. I've done something crazy, something hard, something even I didn't know for certain I could succeed in. And I did it with what felt like an entire community, all of us yearning for freedom, for wellness, for peace. We did it together.

That's why, I think. That's why. I wipe away my remaining tears as we take a bow.

Healing Your Physical Voice

Have you ever lost your voice? Developed a case of laryngitis, when you could only speak in a froggy or whispered tone, if at all? As a singer and teacher, I try to protect my own voice and those of my students from this frustrating and disabling condition. Even today, you won't find me yelling anywhere or trying to speak above a loud crowd without a microphone (or bullhorn). Whenever I have a lot of speaking or singing to do, I take breaks, drink liquids, and make time to sigh and laugh. It's true! Producing sounds in the same (usually low) register for long periods of time can cause your vocal cords to get fatigued. It's a little like only doing sit-ups for your entire workout; your body and your voice do better when you vary which muscles you exercise.

The vocal folds, or 'cords', are not muscles, though; they are small and tender membranes that stretch–long and thin for higher sounds, and shorter and fat for low ones–and vibrate when you open your throat and apply pressurized air to them, like a bow to a violin string. I sometimes remind my students that the voice is a *string* instrument, not a *percussion* instrument. All that talk about "hitting the notes" does not help.

Fun fact: your vocal membranes don't have nerve endings, which is why even when you lose your ability to make sound, it may not hurt at all. The pain you may feel is around them: in the tissue of the pharynx, or in your larynx, the complex "voice box" of muscle and cartilage protecting your vocal folds.

When your cords get stressed–whether due to an illness, overuse, drinking alcohol, taking the wrong medicine, or even during your menstrual period–it can cause the vessels in the vocal folds to swell up. Like fat little sausages, they can't vibrate very well until they shrink to their healthy size. The only real way for that to happen is to rest. Just rest. Yes, you can drink tea, gargle salt water, and inhale steam, that helps. But just being quiet is the best way to recover from laryngitis. To rest. That's right: rest.

For support in the power of resting, visit one of my favorite online sites for womanist theology: The Nap Ministry. Founded by activist, author, and theologian Tricia Hersey, whose bestselling book *Rest is Resistance* promotes resting, touching on the Biblical idea of Sabbath, to push back against our "grind culture." Yes, raising our voices and expressing liberating ideas creates counter-cultural movement, and so does saying "no" and simply stopping, resting, being quiet. Sometimes stopping, doing "nothing," can itself be a powerful act of self-care and healing.

Healing Your Soul Voice

I cannot count the number of women who come to me for voice lessons, having lost their natural head voices from speaking in an unnaturally low and pressed timbre for years just to be taken seriously. Behind many a voice that has lost its power, its openness and confidence, hides the influence of someone–be it a music teacher, family member, or other authority figure–who had told this precious human to "tone it down." Told them that their voice, who they were, was too much, overpowering, even ugly. In cases like these, the major obstacle we first surmount when we begin our work together is rewriting that negative message into a story that affirms their glorious, authentic voice-hood. Freedom.

Other types of oppression directly impact our voices as well– physically, psychologically, and emotionally. How fascinating to note that the chakra[1] associated with power, expression and truth is in, you guessed it, the throat.

Indications of a block in your throat chakra can include chronic sore throat, difficulty with self-expression, and fear of speaking up. These symptoms may be caused, in part, by unprocessed grief, repressed emotions, trauma, and shame.

In the year before I finally left an abusive marriage, the weight of constant oppression found its way into my vocal cords, making them swollen and unresponsive. All those years of playing small; of holding my tongue and my truth, had constricted my voice to the point that I literally burst a blood vessel on my vocal folds. My voice was trying so hard to keep me safe, and it just got tired out and gave up.

Along with an angel of an otolaryngologist, who somehow got me in for surgery that I had no insurance to afford, my healing began with a counselor. Gradually, lightly at first, I related to this counselor my story of emotional and physical abuse at the hands of another singer, the tenor to whom I was married. First, I had to come to terms with the word "abuse."

---

1. Sanskrit for "wheel," the seven centers for energy in the body according to the Hindu Tantric system

Along with countless stereotypes by which I judged my own identity, I held the media-driven idea that only certain people experienced abuse. Not me. No. I attended graduate school, and didn't have a black eye; never had I had to go to the hospital with broken bones (ok, there was that one time). When the counselor shared with me the common pattern of abuse–in a cycle, a repeating circle, over months, years, or a lifetime–I suddenly recognized my own experience. This, at last, gave me the language I needed, not only to refer to my marriage, but also to my child-hood, during which I witnessed my own father punish my mother for her big voice. I saw how as a child I had borne the brunt of mom's uncertainty and fear and dad's sadness and anger. I scratched the surface of understanding my hypervigilance: habitu-ally watching out for any signs of trouble, so that I could keep myself and others safe. I began to understand and heal from my complex trauma. Maybe you have, too. Ask yourself today: is your voice tired from keeping you safe?

Behind my veneer of humor, joy, and encouragement, I hid a lot of fear. That, friends, did not support a career in the performing arts or any other kind of full and liberated life. I felt a certain amount of relief when I finally left New York City, moved away from continually focusing on my resume, from constantly auditioning, from rehearsing while trying to raise a little boy and work full time. Yet even now, thousands of miles and years away from my former life, the hounds of fear still come stalking; espe-cially when I'm tuckered or stressed, it flares up like an old injury. Of course it does.

I'm not talking about stage fright; that's merely the adrenaline we require for any extraordinary feat, be it singing or speaking or running a race. What I feel is more a fear of being found out, revealed as my full self, warts and blessings and all. Sometimes we refer to this as imposter syndrome: that feeling we do not deserve, haven't earned, or cannot sustain our happiness and success. The dirty secret that so many of us hide, fearing that others will discover who we really are and run for the hills. Well, friend, I'm here to tell you: that's some bullshit. I see you. I hear you. I'm here with you and I ain't going nowhere. Truth.

At times like those, it helps to remember the poem by Marianne Williamson, often attributed to Nelson Mandela from his inaugural speech. You may have heard or read it before; try taking a moment, right now, to read this out loud:

> Our deepest fear is not that we are inadequate.
> Our deepest fear is that we are powerful beyond measure.
> It is our light, not our darkness
> That most frightens us.. .
> Your playing small
> Does not serve the world.
> There's nothing enlightened about shrinking
> So that other people won't feel insecure around you.

Be large. Our liberation frees others.

Little Boxes

When you're a Black actress, the box that we often get put in is so small. And me being a dark-skinned Black actress, the opportunities become so limited in a way that is just wrong... It comes down to whether or not I'm given the opportunity to do it.

— *KiKi Layne*

Have you ever felt your identity being molded or constricted by unseen forces into a shape that was not *you,* and wondered who prescribed this shape, this box, as the correct and normal vessel needed for you to "fit in"?

Some of you might remember that song by American folk/blues singer and political activist, Melvina Reynolds, "Little Boxes." (You may best know it as the theme song from the television series *Weeds.*)

Little boxes on the hillside
Little boxes made of ticky-tacky
Little boxes on the hillside
Little boxes all the same...

And the people in the houses
All went to the university
Where they were put in boxes
And they came out all the same...

Can you think of examples of the boxes you've been placed in? How did you adjust your person to fit into them? Did they make you feel safe? Did they hurt you in any lasting way?

65

Some clear examples of harmful boxes are the dangerous trends in women's fashion across place and time that force women's bodies (and presence) to be smaller, such as footbinding in China, and Victorian undergarments in Western Europe and the United States. An article written for the Royal College of English Surgeons[2] describes how the restrictions on women's bodies from tight fitting corsets, fashionable (especially as a sign of class) in the 18th through early 20th century, caused a host of health problems. Women experienced everything from difficulty breathing and fainting to digestive illnesses and permanent deforming of the ribcage. Forced confinement causes lasting damage to humans, in so many ways.

Take just a moment and think of all the boxes society uses to contain humans, and the harm it has done to individuals and communities over time. Mass incarceration and solitary confinement, disproportionately exacted on BIPOC; the destructive stereotypes of racism and homophobia inflicted through physical, social, and legislative constraints; limitations of health, income, and respect placed on those living with different physical and neurological abilities. The list goes on.

What boxes were you raised in? How did they change you, on the outside and on the inside? Are you still in them? Is it time now to bust on out? Perhaps boxes that once fit your identity no longer make sense for you. Imagine shedding them with the joy and relief of taking off your bra at the end of a long day!

Additionally, think of how your voice has changed over the years. Who I am and how I sound has transformed repeatedly over time, responding not only to my age, hormones, and wisdom at any stage of life, but also shaped by those I trusted to coach my singing and speaking at a particular time. We often give so much of our

---

2. The dangers of tight lacing: the effects of the corset — Royal College of Surgeons

power away to those with authority. Heck, I took vows that do that. Even those who mentor us, especially in our capitalist society, can inadvertently place our voices (sound, body, abilities, etc.) into specific categories. In their efforts to make us more marketable, these authorities wind up depriving the very systems they serve of the gifts needed to better adapt, innovate, survive, and thrive.

As a singer, I identify as a lyric soprano, the kind of classical upper voice that portrays many women who die of tuberculosis at the end of the opera (while still singing, poor dears). Famous performing examples in this vocal category include of course the fiery and tragic diva Maria Callas, the late great Jessye Norman, and National Medal of Arts winner Renee Fleming. (For an example of a gorgeous mezzo soprano voice, check out the talented activist, Denyce Graves).[3] My greatest vocal hero, though, is Leontyne Price. In a videotaped interview Diva Price said this: "I have been blessed with a voice that is, even to me, breathtakingly beautiful...I do not apologize for that. My voice is beauty, my voice is America, my voice is my blackness, my voice is love...". Yes, dear diva, it is.

During my own years of development, various teachers made their own guesses about which vocal category I belonged in: one thought I should sing dramatic mezzo (think Delilah to Sampson); still another thought of me as a dramatic coloratura (think Queen of the Night); then there was the mixed category of lyric coloratura (characters whose names often end in handy diminutives like -ina or -etta, equipped with both sexy lyric singing and flashy high passages). With so much to choose from, why choose, you might ask?

All these categories originated in German opera houses, where singers were classified into specific *fachs* (translated "compartments") and given contracts exclusively for roles in that *fach*. I

---

3. www.thedenycegravesfoundation.org

suppose this cut down on arguments about who would sing which role. However, unless you are singing opera in Germany, these categories are not entirely helpful. For much of my adult life, I've been letting other people dictate what I sang and how I sang it. You know what I have to say about that now? *Fach* them!

There seems to be no end of the categorizing we use to place people and their identities into the size and shape of boxes that we can understand. Identities that comply with a certain cultural norm, whether in gender, orientation, race, you name it. Most often, those norms conform to an ideal created and promoted by white, straight, resourced, and cisgender men.

To be clear: there is no shame in adapting to survive. There is even a certain comfort about some restrictions; after all, putting up bumpers in the bowling alley helps with getting lots of strikes and no gutter balls. The Church itself has produced some beautiful art, music, and social services within the structure of rules and boxes. However, the temptation to hold stringently to the narrow definitions of bygone eras, even past the point when they are no longer lifegiving, certainly causes harm.

When I worked as a musician in large, Protestant churches on the East Coast–large enough to afford soloists–most often the medieval holdover of a male, Anglophile ideal defined the music. As a symbol of wealth and status, they venerated either a men and boys' choir, or one in which grown ass women were asked to sound like young boys. I tried, because I needed the money. Now, no thanks.

Later, when I trained to become an Episcopal priest (ancient systems, more progressive theology), boxes abounded. Everything I did, used, wore, each came with a stained-glass word and protocol. Everything from my clothing to my collar to the words referring to me originated with a male role model, even though women have been ordained since 1976 (and LGB folx right afterward, in 1977).

After nearly 50 years to adapt, folx still often query, "what do I *call* you?"

"Well," I regularly reply, "what did you call your last priest (rector or vicar)?"

"Um, Father Bill."

Then comes the tricky part.

"Well, you might like to call me 'Mother Joyce' then." And upon sensing their discomfort I add, "My nickname is MoJo. Some people find that easier." Children love my nickname. I think it helps them build a bridge between who I am and how they already perceive I'm expected to be.

Very recently, a highly respected friend and colleague, Deacon Vicki Gray, the first openly transgender person ordained in the Diocese of California in 2006, passed away at the age of 86. Prior to both her transition and ordination, Vicki served for years in the U.S. Navy and in the U.S. Foreign Service. After her ordination, she served several churches and communities in the Bay Area. She and her lifelong love remained married through her gender-affirming transition, perplexing those who held tightly to a certain image of human relationships.

Rev. Vicki is featured in a short documentary entitled *Voices of Witness: Out of the Box*[4], produced by IntegrityUS. In this video, created in 2012, Vicki talks about the difficulties she experienced in coming out of her gender box while participating in the Church.

Certain sweeping societal traumas can nevertheless break open and expose unhelpful, irrelevant boxes. The recent COVID epidemic revealed the vast disconnect between institutional biases and the needs of the world. Our current national (and global) climate of brutally enforcing outdated prejudices is causing (hopefully) many folx to examine and discard harmful human categorization. Did you experience any of these cracks in the institutions

---

4. Voices of Witness: Out of the Box

of which you are a part? Perhaps now is a good time to go on in and make yourself heard.

I wonder: what would it feel, sound, look like for you to speak into a room of white, cis, heteronormative humans using your soaring, or sultry, or sassy, and sparklingly true voice, wearing the shapes and colors of your heart, and choosing your own name? Let's try this exercise:

Take a moment right now; pick up some paper—a journal, a sketch pad, even the margins of this book—and something to write with: colored pencil, crayon, pen. Without thinking too much about it (you might choose to use your non-dominant hand for this), draw the shape of your voice. Not only a literal representation of your own body, but your essence, your power, the sound and image of YOU. What does it look like? Sound like? Feel like? Does it have a name or title? I'll bet it doesn't fit into a box, does it?

Bodies in a Box

Hmmm. What does that remind you of?

Our physical appearances and the colonizing impact on our identities intersect with the issue of body image and ideals. Transgender humans might struggle with gender dysphoria and certainly benefit from space and support during their transition to their true gender expression. Gender non-binary humans assert a place for their identity outside of limiting norms. Ironically, even though the expressions of non-binary humans seem to cause distress to those well within current gender norms, strict gender expectations harm humans both within and between these constructed and inorganic categories.

As someone who's been through childbirth twice, I can tell you: averages are meaningless statistics when it comes to producing a human life. No two births are the same in length of time, or process, in feeling or outcomes. By boiling down individual birth stories into conglomerate averages, the medical industry has increased the number of dangerous interventions and C-section deliveries (up from 4.5% to over 32% nationally during my lifetime). We induce women to fit their birthing into financially expedient averages, when providing patient (two meanings) care and listening to individual stories and needs results in more powerful mothers and healthier outcomes.

How has your own body changed during your lifetime, and has it conformed to the "average" during those transformations? I know that, as a cisgender female human in my 60s, my body has been through many phases: my muscular and lithe young adulthood, my soft and nourishing motherhood, and my now bolder post-menopause physique. None of these ever completely squared with the conflicting ideals for my attractiveness, lovability, and professional success.

What's the famous saying, "until the fat lady sings"? While Bugs Bunny cartoons epitomise the stereotype of buxom operatic women in breast plates, à la Wagner's *Ring Cycle*, in the real life world of competitions and casting dictates, especially among female singers (like many other "me too" professions), a svelte, beauty-pageant ideal ruled the day. It's a bind.

I've struggled with my weight for most of my adult life. During times when my relationship with food took on unhealthy proportions (either bingeing or strict dieting), at least a part of this emotional landscape came from my response to complex and often contradicting cultural expectations about my body. My desire to become weightless, bound with my need to weigh myself down to

Joyce Parry Moore

stay safe. For more about these patterns, I invite you to read the at one time groundbreaking (and slightly dense) research of Marion Woodman, especially *The Owl was a Baker's Daughter*. [5]

For years, my body felt like the property of the male gaze, its main purpose to entertain, amuse, arouse. It did not seem like my own. Even when I sang Madama Butterfly, my most demanding vocal and acting role (albeit a culturally appropriating one, for which I apologize) one of my concerns at the time was to lose enough weight so that the tenor could carry me down the aisle after my suicide. Seriously, Joyce? Meanwhile my voice teacher worried that my newly thin body would no longer be able to support my voice.

Do you ever vacillate between impossible physical ideals? (For a moving expression of this from a woman's perspective, check out America Ferrera's monologue in the *Barbie Movie*.) Would you love to chuck these false and contradicting standards and simply adore the body you live in, right now? Go on! Do it! Your body will teach you if you listen. And when we don't listen, it speaks more loudly.

What might your body be saying to you now, if you listen? Is your strong bone structure crying out to be recognized for carrying you this far? Is your skin–dappled, wrinkled, scarred–asking you to honor its resilience and history? Are your genitals–new, old, transformed–demanding affirmation and protection? Take a moment to thank your body for all it has done for you for all these years. Pay attention to the relationship you have with your physical self. Where are you?

Even at this stage in my physical and emotional development, before a recent concert I tried out some Spanx to smooth out my waistline. Yup, ye olde support garments, alive and well. Ironically,

5. The Owl was a Baker's Daughter: Obesity, Anorexia Nervosa and the Repressed ... - Marion Woodman - Google Books

although it did create a slimmer silhouette in my now form-fitting dress, my belly was unable to release enough while wearing it to draw a full breath or engage my abdominals that support my voice.

On the night of the performance, I stood in front of a mirror, and my youngest daughter (who uses they/them pronouns), now 26 and a theater costumer, beamed at me and exclaimed, "You look so beautiful, mom. I'm so proud of you!"

"Really? Even with this old belly?" I patted my post-menopause pooch.

"Especially with your belly! I love every part of you. It all tells your beautiful story."

This remarkable human, born from my body when I was a "geriatric" 38 years old, has blossomed into a fierce and talented force in the world. Beholding them and knowing some of their stories of resilience, I feel a wave of gratitude. Partly because I realized that by sharing the truth of my story with them, I gave this child of mine permission to tell their story, to love themselves as full humans. Ari and their generation inspire me to do better.

Despite—perhaps in resistance to—the current national drive to reverse growth in creativity and diversity, Ari is earning their graduate degree in Arts Leadership, combining their skills in theatre and gender studies. They dream of founding their own theatre company, dedicated to amplifying the narratives and talents of marginalized people. They've taught me so much about the origins of gender roles and the importance of rejecting false binaries. They inspire me (and often gently correct me) every day with their brave and true living and give me hope that human beings are indeed evolving beyond our heteronormative past.

What do current generations of artists, activists, and leaders teach you? How might you amplify, support, and collaborate with them?

P.S. I discarded the Spanx and crushed the concert.

Different Abilities

Part of our evolution as human creatures includes honoring our physical experiences. Beyond the tyranny of words and punctuation, our bodies and their variety of senses give us lots of other information that can be shared in our storytelling. These sensory experiences create a visceral connection between the storyteller and the hearer. Think about significant stories you've heard being spoken, acted, sung, etc. Are there smells that convey the meaning of their words? Colors? Tastes? A change in temperature or the quality of light?

For some humans, and for all of us at some point in our lives, one or more of our senses may become temporarily or permanently disabled. Friends who suffered the effects of Long COVID still struggle coping with a new way of life, one without senses of smell or taste, or perhaps even the energy to walk without assistance. As we grow older, our vision and our hearing often change, which in turn impacts the way we live our lives, and may even cause us to strengthen and rely upon our other senses to make meaning in the world.

Latinx painter Frida Kahlo became disabled in her early adulthood by a terrible bus accident. She underwent dozens of surgeries throughout her lifetime, and long, painful periods of recovery. Yet, Kahlo embraced her broken body, as it was, as a part of her identity and her art, and forged new thoughts about creativity, gender, and disablement.[6] Rather than accepting the imposed limitations of a colonizing box describing what she could do and be, Kahlo lay in her bed and painted, showing us a new vision of beauty, one that includes wounds, scars, and limitations.

---

6. Using the word "disablement", rather than disability, here indicates the process of living with a long-term or short-term impairment of one's physical or mental abilities. It makes fluid the solid notion of "disability", or being "disabled".

By painting herself dissected by braces, and in the throes of her several miscarriages, Kahlo showed us "a new way of experiencing pain", as "a way to position herself in the world" (Betcher, pg. 183). In her book *Spirit and the Politics of Disablement,* Sharon Betcher exposes the way our consumer-driven society distances us from bodies and from pain, until we "stand outside of the flesh, in a vast commodification of reality...that eventually turns [our] bodies into things in need of modification and perfection."[7]

What if your voice, your body, your identity no longer included the colonizing notion of perfection? What if your body's particular abilities and disabilities became a source of wisdom for all that you create? What if your own blessed flesh became part of your calling in the world? What senses do you rely upon to position your voice in your current context?

Theatre designers communicate with a variety of senses to help tell the story of the playwright and actors: the shapes, colors, and textures of the set; the quality of the lights; perhaps adding other sounds or music. Canadian playwright John Murrell includes smells in his plays to convey intimate knowledge: cooking huevos rancheros during *The Faraway Nearby*, about Georgia O'Keeffe; and having real soil on stage in the set of *Democracy*, a story about a fictional meeting between Ralph Waldo Emerson and Walt Whitman in the American Civil War.

Which sensory experiences cause you to pause, shiver, sigh, or cry out, as they carry a voice or story into your very bones, your inner being? And which of those senses might you engage as you tell your own story with your own voice? Let's ask ourselves: in what ways do we connect physically with one another's stories?

---

7. Betcher, Sharon, *Spirit and the Politics of Disablement,* pg. 182 & 183, quoting Sarah Lowe and Linda Holler

Resonance

Have you ever said to someone, "That really resonates with me"? Did you stop to think about the scientific phenomenon behind that statement? Whenever you speak, sing, or play an instrument the sound disturbs the air, creating vibrations of various frequencies. These vibrations travel through the space you're in and connect with other surfaces: walls, windows, membranes in our ears, even our bones. When you tell your story, the vibration literally touches other people and things around you. Your voice "re-sounds" in ever expanding sonic and emotional ripples.

Vibration—energy, sound, or light waves formed into words, color, or movements—can change the patterns around us, can create new realities. Many creation myths from various global traditions refer to the power of vibration. For example, in the Hindu story of the beginnings of life, a great river of vibration begets all living beings; in the Judeo-Christian Genesis story, the Divine voice heralds life—"And G*d said, let there be light." These stories resonate with humans across time and place, repeated in the physical sensation of chanting and singing songs of gratitude. In our souls, humans long to join a "vibe" of expansiveness and unity.

I viscerally learned the power of vibration in storytelling when performing opera for deaf children. Boston Lyric Opera's education outreach program hired me to sing in their children's production of "The Goose Girl," a vocal telling of that rather Grimm, German fairy tale, composed by contemporary American composer Thomas Pasatieri. This production made special efforts to be accessible to children who lived with hearing loss.

Each performer teamed with a partner who signed everything we sang; they even interacted with us and shared our characters' emotional experiences. At the same time, each hearing-impaired child in the audience held an inflated balloon, through which they could feel the vibrations created by our voices.

How about you? Have you ever experienced being at the theatre, or concert hall, or in a restaurant or living room, listening intently to a voice conveying a powerful story, and had it literally vibrate in your body, give you what my southern friends refer to as "chill bumps"? If such a stirring physical and emotional connection of sound and story, creator and listener, causes a change in you, in me, can it also resonate out into the world? Is this a physical conveyance of empathy? How do we nurture such connections, rather than ignore or shut down this at times unsettling mystery? Can we evolve in our understanding and make room for forward movement?

Colleen's Story: The Singing Gondolier

Growing up, I loved to sing. Even better, I knew I COULD sing! "You have a beautiful voice," they told me. Ahh, external validation, that double-edged sword! The problem with relying on external validation for your voice comes when, as you start to pay attention to the voices around you, you begin the game of comparison. You notice the beautiful ones, and you want your voice to sound like them, because now you have expectations to fill, and you don't want to let anyone down. And you start to crave another hit of that sweet nectar, those compliments, that applause. I became overly aware of the fact that one of my friends could make up harmonies in her head, and another one could riff on the fly. I could do no such things. I just wasn't good enough.

In my quest, I joined church choirs and school choirs–I even auditioned for the "gifted and talented" music program at school. But the voices around me were growing ever so much sweeter, while mine was becoming more constricted. I began to feel what I call the hand of Vulnerability fasten around my larynx and every time I compared myself to one of the singing angels around me, Vulnerability clenched her fist, and I felt like I was strangling. Singing publicly (especially a solo) became a struggle. Everything felt tight, like my voice was stuck in my throat.

My parents knew I wanted to perform for my career. At first, I focused mainly on ballet and acting. So, they decided I could round that out with some voice lessons. Joyce lived near my family, and my mother knew her from the community. Shortly after my father died, I began studying voice with Joyce. Our work together during my high school years, during a time of trauma and loss, had a lasting impact on my life.

As an incoming freshman, I auditioned for Concert Choir, and I didn't get in. The band director (who was also the choir director, and that's probably all you need to know about his knowledge of the voice) rejected me. He impressed upon me this idea that I couldn't hold pitch. He loomed over me at the piano as this intimidating figure spouting off about what the other girls in the choir were capable of, and how I just wasn't good enough. It was Joyce who one day made a throwaway comment while I was singing Mabel from the Pirates of Penzance for her: "You have great natural pitch," she said, and at once I felt Vulnerability loosen her grip.

It's not lost on me that I was letting many critical adults dictate how I felt about myself. That's what you do when you're a teenager, right? Do teachers and parents ever truly understand the great responsibility they hold in mentoring young people? Joyce did. She was always nurturing and kind. My voice grew and flourished with her. More importantly, my confidence did. She taught me life lessons about how to be a woman and a human being.

One day, I showed up to my lesson unprepared. Instead of reaming me, which would happen to me by other voice teachers in later years, Joyce stopped the lesson when she could see I was close to tears, and had me show her my calendar. Then she started helping me to cross items out of my overloaded schedule. She encouraged me to say "no" to things I thought I should do, out of obligation, but that in fact were stealing my energy and my joy. It was the first time someone showed me how to form boundaries. Fifteen years later, my therapist repeated this when she, too, had me hand over my calendar, and asked me to practice saying "no" to something for my homework. By this time, at the age of 43, after a little practice, I have finally learned this lesson.

When I submitted my audition tape for All-Southeast Honor Choir, I had to give it to the dreaded band director. He pulled me aside, and told me the tape was such a travesty, that he couldn't possibly submit it, and we would have to re-record. Again, something about my pitchy-ness. I think when I started crying, and we had to record the entire tape through my tears, he felt bad.

But I think (hope) he felt even worse when I was crowned 1st chair 2nd soprano in all of SE Alaska! Because I noticed after that moment, he didn't fuck with me anymore. No more talk of me not being able to hold pitch. He tried to be like, "Aren't you glad we re-recorded?" But Joyce and I have a theory that he sent in the first tape, because in the second one, I am literally snotting and snuffling my way through it. It was as if those judges–those outside, expert opinions on MY singing–had influenced HIS opinion about ME.

The result for me was that I wasn't scared of him anymore, and I got to sing solos, and have a nice part in the high school musical, and everything was good. But WHY did it even have to start out like that? Why was it necessary for me, as a woman (a girl of 14, really) to have to prove myself to some man in a position of authority over me, to gain his respect?

Those early, compassionate voice lessons so importantly unbound my voice, and gave it the freedom to soar again. Would I still make comparisons as I entered college and became a vocal *performance major? Absolutely. Would future abusive teachers and negative experiences lock me up again? Yes. And then I became a gondolier.*

You read that right: toward the end of college in Nevada, I took a job as a gondolier at the Venetian Hotel. Oddly there, recalling the freedom I'd experienced in my lessons as a young person, I rediscovered my confidence. I didn't have a choice! We were out on the water, singing 2-3 arias per gondola, fifteen times a day. That's A LOT of singing. There's no accompaniment, no warm-up, and no resting on days when you're in "bad voice." And guess what? People loved it! It didn't matter if I made a mistake or wasn't perfect—they didn't care! I learned to stop being so damn critical of myself.

Now when people are like, "Sing something, I want to hear some opera, you singing monkey, you!" I don't even hesitate, I'm not weird about it like I used to be. I don't care, I just get back on that boat, mentally. I'll blurt out whatever they want. So share your gift with the world! It doesn't have to be perfect to be great!

I went on to have a touring career in musical theatre, performing for audiences around the world (and not in any boats). What an adventure! During this time, I remembered something else Joyce told me, probably before I was ready to hear it: "Whatever happens, guard your flame. That passion deep in your heart that drives your creativity. People may try to extinguish it sometimes. Don't you let them!" Heard, Chef. I didn't.

Eventually, I settled into another life, one with a loving husband and two complex children with their own neuro-spiciness and gender expressions. I've become an advocate for workers' rights and for humans with learning differences. Who knows what tomorrow will bring? But I know this. No one, but no one, gets to tamp down my flame, or silence my voice. I know who I am, and my gondola is on the move!

Some Practical Advice

You may not have access to a gondola to practice your vocal strength. And you undoubtedly face many opportunities to explore and develop your newfound lightsaber. Let's check in.

What happens when you speak in public? I mean for you, physically and emotionally. In *your* body: do you feel authentic and grounded? Or does the hand of "vulnerability" begin to choke you? Do you focus on the center of your being and the veracity of your message, or do you think about the ears of those listening (or sometimes not), and wonder whether you are meeting their expectations or comparing favorably to others? Does your voice, your means of expression, feel free to say what it needs in the way, the register, the volume that is authentic for you? Next time you're speaking, and you notice a disconnect between your voice and your body, your words and your meaning, I invite you to take a pause. Let silence hold things for a moment.

In that moment, connect with your breath. Feel the way it fills your body, your belly, down through your toes. Feel your toes on the ground, wiggle them, and sense the rootedness that supports you. You can even stretch your soft palate (like yawning), expand your ribcage, and then audibly sigh–*Ahhhhh!*–just to experience the power, the breadth, the vibration of your own personhood, your own unique voice. Then, start again. You've got this!

Practice Makes (semi) Permanent

Of course, it helps to practice. Someone once told me, "Practice doesn't make perfect, practice makes permanent." In other words, practices–whether it's a new way to speak, or move, or write–develop new patterns of belief and behavior in our muscle memory and brain synapses. We now know that the brain retains its plasticity–its ability to change, to try new things–long into our lives. We're not done by age 5, as used to be the wisdom. Turns out, you *can* teach an old dog new tricks. Woof!

In music, there is an expression about staying in shape to make your best, strongest sound. We can call it our "chops." This can refer to anything from the muscles that wind instrument players train in their mouth to produce their tone, to the dexterity in a pianist's fingers and arms that allow fluid playing, or to the flexibility of expression for public speakers. Like any physical endeavor, this takes daily practice.

Keep in mind that the amount you practice depends on your "instrument." As a freshman voice major in college, I enthusiastically signed up for a practice room every single day. I noticed that the piano or violin majors around me practiced for hours on end, so I endeavored to do the same. At first. Then I discovered that when I sang for more than an hour it hurt more than helped. Voice is the only instrument that you "play" from the inside out, with your throat containing the "strings" of your instrument. I gained greater respect for my physical instrument, limited my vocal practice to one-hour sessions, and spent my other hours practicing dance, theatre, and language instead. You have the right to honor your own limits. That takes practice, too.

Practicing Boundaries

Especially as women or other subordinated voices, conditioned by culture to please others above all else, we might need to practice saying certain things. Like "no." Complete sentence. No explanation necessary. Rosa Parks changed the world with that one-word sentence–NO–when she refused to give up her seat on a Montgomery bus. Setting boundaries is a powerful action. Your "no" can change your relationship, your vocation, and the systems to which you belong.

Once you're more comfortable with that one word approach, you can also practice saying, "I'm still talking" when someone interrupts you. When you're feeling even stronger, you might try saying, "When you did/said that I felt unsafe/unheard/sad/angry/etc." Just a statement of your feelings. No need to explain; no invitation to argue. Just the facts.

What are the phrases you would like to practice so that you can say them with strength and ease?

Not only setting but following through on boundaries can be one of the most challenging and most rewarding practices for any voice placed on the margins. We've been taught, time and again, that our identity and our worth depend upon serving everyone else and abiding by the rules that are set *for* us, not *by* us, and very often without our input or representation. Legislatures limiting women's rights to manage their own reproductive health include few if any women in the room. Laws prohibiting medical support for transgender youth are made without input from the youth themselves, often by lawmakers with little to no understanding of gender expression beyond an outdated binary. The false belief that we do not have the right to self-sovereignty over our own bodies paves the way for other kinds of abuse.

In cases of abuse—physical, psychological, sexual—the very first step of that assault is the violation of our personal and physical boundaries. Our "no" is not heeded, our physical limits are not respected. The deep-seated trauma of abuse can cause effects lasting years or lifetimes following the incident.

In the 2025 independent film *Sorry, Baby,* writer/director/actor Eva Victor portrays a young woman who is sexually assaulted by her thesis advisor at a fictional liberal arts college in rural New England. For years following the attack, her character,

Agnes, struggles with the confidence to act and make choices in her life. Eventually, with the support of friends, their baby, and a cat, Agnes begins to connect again with her own story and emotions.

When we learn to set and maintain personal boundaries over concrete, measurable things like our health care, use of our time and resources, and choice of actions, we not only strengthen our own integrity and voice, we also possibly inspire those around us, in respecting our boundaries, to begin setting and keeping their own.

Early in my own healing from the abusive relationship that harmed my body, soul, and voice, a theatre where I worked asked me to perform an extra show in one day, for a role in which I bore much of the vocal and energetic burden. I said "no," and was then confronted by the director, someone I deeply admired. Scary though it was, I explained that I've learned to take care of my body and voice and set boundaries about my limitations, and I stuck to it.

Practice following through on a consequence: say you're leaving work on time and then do it; state your salary and benefit requirements for a job or promotion, and if they are not met, walk away (in the timing that is healthy for you); tell someone that you will not be around sexist, racist, or homophobic jokes, and when they still choose to make them, leave the room or meeting (and report them to HR). What are some boundaries you'd like to set and how committed are you to practicing them?

Good news: you don't need to sign up for a practice room to do this! We have opportunities every day: in meetings, classrooms, families, companies, demonstrations, performances. You can also practice with your body–how you love it, hold it, respect it–and other forms of expression. Think of the posture you'd like to use when you say "no!" Statistics show that adopting a confident body posture–stretched spine, grounded feet, intentional gestures, eye contact–can help overcome anxiety and instill a positive mindset. Find fellow revolutionaries who can practice together with you!

Find a mentor

It also helps to have guidance and support along the way, someone to coach you on finding and practicing the voice that fully resonates as yours. This may take some searching. Find someone whom you trust with that most vulnerable part of you, someone skilled in their art, and (and this is important) who wants you to sound like YOU, not a copy of them.

I recall clearly when a voice student of mine asked me in all honesty, "How did you become who you are? I want to be, well, I want to be *you!*"

"Why would you want to be anyone other than your beautiful self?" I asked them in return.

An expert and supportive mentor will meet you where you are, acknowledge your strengths, clarify your goals, and help you build the skills to achieve your growth. I used to think that a good teacher needed to be hard on me; I've studied with people who called me names, made me cry, even one who put their fingers in my mouth with no warning. Yuck! These teachers had no idea of my history, my identity, my skills, or my life goals. They didn't believe that my story had any significance in my education.

Education, from the Latin word *educare*, means "to draw forth" knowledge from another human. In the age of colonialism, education came to mean merely depositing wisdom, then to hear it echoed back verbatim in tests and performances. Revolutionary educator Paulo Freire termed this style of teaching "banking pedagogy," a tool of oppression. Conversely, when we contextualize learning to draw forth the inherent wisdom in a student or client, this kind of pedagogy can and does start revolutions. I'm so there for that! I hope you are too.

Oppressive teaching structures can lead to an abuse of power (hence, Mr. Mouth Prober, or MMP). They take for granted the sacred privilege of working with the most holy, most intimate parts of someone's personal identity. Sometimes they go so far as to weaponize it for their own self-aggrandizement. No thank you, MMP! We've got better things to do.

Once you find someone, invest your (boundaried) time, your energy, even your money, because...you * are * worth * it! In such a partnership, you will ignite your determination for daily practice, for coming to the page or the canvas or the instrument, even when you don't really feel like it, and the courage to notice what works that day and what still needs work.

How shall we work, you might ask? There are as many ways as there are voices; allow me here to invite you into some introductory exercises. While they are focused on vocalizing, I think you'll find that they bring other strengths as well.

Some Exercises: Breath, Ease, Expansion, Support, and Vision

Since singing is my thang, let me share some metaphors and physical exercises from that discipline that may inspire you as you find your own voice, physically, emotionally, and spiritually.

First: breathe. Breathe, breathe, breathe. If nothing else, singing (or writing or dancing) puts you in touch with a greater portion of your body and life energy. Most people, most days, go around like they're carrying their brain in a jar on a broom handle. Your brain is part of a complex and expansive nervous system. Physical investment in expression, in the creation of our own life, demands and gives you a sense of your breath, your blood, your muscles and bones. It literally helps to calm and align your nervous system.

Every time you begin some creative endeavor—writing, speaking, singing—begin with some breaths. In through your nose to a count of 4 or 5, feeling the air fall into your body and filling all three lobes of your lungs, bottom, to middle, to top. Take just a bit of a pause—another 4 count—at the top of the breath, and sit on that pillow of air, as though you were preparing to meditate on a cushion. Then release the air, slowly—perhaps through pursed lips or even making a puffing or a hissing sound—to the count of another 4 or 5. Feel that compressed breath leave your body, your lungs fully empty, and allow your shoulders to hang loosely, and your sternum to lift, as though suspended from the heavens on a string. Imagine lifting and even expanding your ribcage. I invite you to repeat this cycle several times, pausing briefly before each repetition. Note: as always, feel empowered to adapt any physical practice for your unique circumstances.

Next, Ease. Which can seem like an oxymoron. Sure, Joyce: "ease." Yet to find that flow, that voice that belongs to you alone, you must trust your breath and your body and let things go. I like to use the term "ease" rather than that dreaded word "relax" (just writing the word makes me tense). "Relax" is what the doctor tells you before an uncomfortable procedure. *Ease* is what it looks like when an eagle soars, or a sea turtle glides in the water. Sighing helps. I can always tell when my students are in the building, because I heard a lot of sighing going on! Lilting Ahhhhhs or

Helloooos (à la Mrs. Doubtfire). Any Zen-like practice–be it singing, or running, or skiing, or swimming, or something else–balances effort with ease. Picture a duck swimming in the lake: on the surface they glide with ease, and beneath that ease their feet paddle away.

To find your ease, you can try following Tay Tay's advice and "shake it off!" I mean it! Stand with your sternum lifted, and your feet shoulder width apart. Begin by gently shaking your head–gentle side to side nos (good practice for those boundaries!) and little up and down yeses. Then, let your jaw unhinge. Just easily, not with the force of a boa constrictor before a meal! Practice a slack jaw pose, like "duh!" With that loose jaw, shake your head again, allowing your lips to flap and blubber away. Then, take a light hold of your chin, and waggle it up and down. It may help to make some noise–buh, buh, buh.
You can even extend the shaking to include your whole body–shoulders, arms, belly, legs–a little like the Hokey Pokey. Maybe that IS what it's all about!

Then Expansion. Expanding your muscles, your bones, your ideas and dreams and colors and gestures. As a singer, actor, preacher, and speaker, my body and my vocal cavity, inside and out, expand beyond what I thought possible. When your voice is lined up and spinning, you will feel both expansive and connected, as though you have melded into something much, much bigger than yourself. Sounds woo woo, I know, but it's true. Let's try it now.

Take a moment to stretch, I mean realllly streeeetch. Luxu-
riously. From your fingers down to your toes. First, reach
your arms up, up, to the heavens and beyond. Allow your
torso to remain still, and stretch your arms up and away
from it, while your shoulders move down from your ears.
Wiggle your fingers and pretend you're trying to pick a deli-
cious apple from a very tall tree. You can almost reach it!
Your feet are still rooted deep in the ground, so the stretch
runs all through your body. After a few moments, allow
your arms to float down, lightly, and reach them out to
either side of your body. (Don't worry, we're not doing any
jumping jacks!) Allowing your feet to stay grounded, feel
your arms reaching in both directions, with the energy
shooting out of your fingertips and shining onto the walls.
You may even let them gently rock you from side to side, as
they take turns reaching in those opposite directions.
Finally, if you're feeling confident, allow your head to
gently stretch down to your chest, and your arms to fold into
your body and give yourself a little squeeze. Release your
arms as your heavy, heavy head leads your body to fold
forward, one vertebra at a time, like a long string of pearls.
Go ahead and bend your softened knees just a bit; this is an
easy stretch. When you've gone as far as comfortable, just
hang there for a moment, like a limp rag doll. Your arms can
go all floppy, and you might gently shake your head in those
little nos and yeses again. When you're ready, allow your-
self to roll back up, just the way you rolled down, with your
head coming up very last. Look at you! You're enormous!

And Support. Perhaps the most mysterious of concepts, in singing and elsewhere. Yes, we breathe with ease and expansion. And. Voice also takes energy; it takes balanced tension. If you've ever practiced yoga, you may have experienced this: we stretch in opposite directions and create a dynamic energy in the body. It's not static. This generates some resistance, some heat, sometimes even anxiety. It may feel uncomfortable until you get used to it. Remember that there is a difference between "natural" and "habitual." You're building new habits that will eventually feel organic.

In singing, we balance the energy it takes to pressurize our breath with the ease in our throat. In speaking, perhaps it's the strength of our message with the ease of our confidence. In life, and relationships, we support ourselves and others through a balance of rigorous honesty and loving compassion. How can you practice this kind of balance in your voice, your healing, and your collaborations? For now, let's return to our breath.

This time, when you take that easy, expansive breath, and sit on that lovely cushion of air, you're going to add just a little gentle pressure. See if you can embody the concept of effort and ease at the same time. As you release your breath, in a long, slow stream—again either with pursed lips or a hiss—stretch your body outward. Feel your ribcage expand all the way around your body, and your sternum gently lifting again. Experience the marvel of expanding even as your breath empties. Try this a few times to feel the balance of it. Now, let's articulate it differently, like a bow on a violin. You can make some strong pulses: with your hand on your tummy (around your solar plexus), feel your breath press against your hand as you say "hey!" or "ha!" Say it

like you mean it. As though someone is in your yard step-
ping on your prized rose bushes. "Hey! Knock it off!" Don't
press on your throat or try to make either a low or high
sound. Just an open sound. With power. "Hey there!"

Whoa. I hear you!

Finally, Vision. That's right. Remember, everything that you
create is created twice: first in your imagination, and then in your
physical reality. Whether you're singing, moving, or painting,
when you breathe in, let that breath become the beauty you imagine—a powerful gesture, an expressive brush stroke, or a lyric
phrase. Once you have that vision in your mind, ears, heart, all that
remains is to enact it—to articulate it in the world.

Take an expansive breath and imagine you're filling a paint
brush with color. (Note: the longer the phrase, or gesture,
the more paint you will need!) Be specific: what color is it?
Azure blue like the horizon? Emerald green like the
towering redwoods? Fiery red like a field of poppies? Now,
use your hand as you would when creating with that brush,
making a gesture that articulates your vision—a long,
sweeping arc, wavy curves or curls, or playful dots and
blotches—and release your breath as you gesture. It may help
if you make some sounds—ha ha ha, or ahhhhhh, or woooo—it
will begin to make the connection for you. Let it become
like a game. Like being a vocal Bob Ross. Have fun!

And More to Explore

Remember my story about learning to vary my approach to vocal practice? Instead of working in the practice room for hours, I exercised my brain and my body in different ways. And you can too! Reading new authors–especially writers on the margins–can birth new visions for you and encourage you to find and strengthen your own voice. Go to a gallery or museum to experience an artist you've never seen before. Listening to podcasts (check out the *Fill the Room Coaching* weekly podcast) can expand your mind and thus your expression and vision.

Take time to experience new things: a new trail, a new landscape; a new country or a new language (I recommend Italian); a new cuisine or type of music or genre of theatre; check out a new band, a new comic, or new performance artist. Whether you love it, hate it, or something in between, expanding your spirit makes more room for your vision and your voice to grow and resonate. Remember, you're stretching and setting your own limits!

The View from Here

Wow. Look how far we've come together! We've explored ways to find and/or rediscover our own, unique voices of expression and power in the world. We've listened deeply to the call of our lives, following our joy and our passion toward new horizons. We've practiced the power of boundaries and learned exercises to expand our breathing and expression. And we've considered ways to practice using our newfound voice, developing it to become stronger, more true, more resonant. What's next?

Remember when we dispelled the notion that "filling the room" is a zero-sum game? I believe that it's more than ok to fill the room–the classroom, the board room, the stage, the streets, the halls of Congress–*along with others*. Your commitment to honing your own voice will make your collaboration more confident! And working in solidarity with like-hearted humans toward a vision that inspires and expands possibilities for marginalized humans, well, it's the best! So, how do we find our people?

During your journey to discover and develop your theme song, you will likely come across groups and individuals with whom you strongly resonate. You've heard stories that inspire you, literally fill you with breath and support and spirit, that heal and free you. You've done that for others, too. Because, friend, when you shine, when you fill the room with your voice–your story, your sound, your expression, your presence–you give others permission to do the same.

This is a new kind of choir: rather than shrinking ourselves and others to blend into a single predetermined ideal, we support one another's strengths to create new and exciting harmonies. The more that we claim our hidden superpowers and speak/sing/dance out, the more we can shift the cultural climate for us and for future generations. So go ahead: take up all the space you need to heal! I'm right here with you.

And it's not only me beside and behind you: right now, millions of other, previously silenced voices want and need to join with you. We need you to use your light and revolutionary resonance as a powerful tool for changing systems and healing lives and communities. Whether you join your voice–speaking, singing, moving, writing–in protest or in affirmation, on the streets or in the classroom, the integrity of even knowing and developing your true voice can and does inspire and motivate others to speak up.

An historically revolutionary term from community organizing is solidarity; *solidaridad.* The word carries complex meaning: unity and fellowship within a community that shares common values and vision, as well as showing support for other communities. Latinx civil rights activist Cesar Chavez famously said "*La gente unida, jamás será vencida,*" translated into English meaning

"People united will never be defeated." And we can be united without being *exactly the same*. As in all of nature, diversity adds to our strength and resilience.

What keeps us quiet is the shame of feeling we don't fit in, that we are alone, that we are in a sub-normal minority. Nope. We jettisoned that baggage pages ago, remember? Full steam ahead!

Let's go find your people and make some noise together. We may get to travel, so pack light.

Third Movement: Connect

One of the most vital ways we sustain ourselves is by building communities of resistance, places where we know we are not alone.

— bell hooks

Dancing Together in the Arctic

THE DANCERS FROM KING ISLAND AND LITTLE DIOMEDE *gather with us inside Nome's high school cafeteria/auditorium. Chaos ensues as we peel off our numerous outer layers—snow pants, parkas, sweaters, hats, gloves—and breathe in the warmth. Outside the temps hover around 40 below zero (Fahrenheit).*

I bring with me a cast of thirty-five singers, dancers, storytellers, crew and instrumentalists, ages 9 to 79, flown from around the country. New Yorkers experiencing Alaska for the first time feel like they've landed on the moon; Alaskan artists on their first Arctic adventure struggle to find their bearings. As for me, I fluctuate between surreal excitement, and overwhelming worry that this will

95

somehow not all work out. Like a mother hen with quite a varied brood to care for, I fret and gather, ineffectually.

I pause to calm myself and take in the group. We embody an impressive spectrum of generations, genders, cultures, perspectives: an Inuit couple in their seventies share stories from their distant childhoods; an Irish tenor from the East Coast stands quietly aloof, wondering perhaps when he'll get paid; children in colorful, hand-made kuspuks trimmed in rickrack chase one another on the squeaky linoleum; a dashing Filipino baritone from Los Angeles shines his charm on some of the elder Inuit women; elderly matri-archs wearing parkas and ancient men holding walrus skin drums regard one another with mutual respect. It's a lot. It's the world.

The Inuit group performs for us first: the women dancing in a line, and the men hitting flat, moon-round drums with long sticks, singing in Inupiat language and tone. Each dance is played twice, first more quietly, and then repeated with a louder, more insistent beat, laid down in pairs, like a slow iamb from Shakespeare's verses: ba BUM, ba BUM, ba BUM. The air vibrates with history and with possibility: remembering the deep sorrow inflicted by early mission-aries who then forbade this dancing for fear of demonic influence; and celebrating the joyful pride of the Inuit people for recovering this cultural rite.

Us Gussuks shyly revere the privilege of the moment. "Gussuk," a somewhat derogatory term for non-Indigenous people, comes from the Yupik word kass'aq, which itself derives from the Eastern European term "Cossack," referring to Russian military, early Alaskan colonizers. Little Diomede, colonized as part of American Alaska, neighbors Big Diomede, colonized by Russia, less than 3 miles away. The Chukchi Sea separates the islands; a world seems to separate we "chechakos" (newcomers to Alaska) from these wisdom bearers.

The King Island dancers then invite everyone into a commu-nity dance. Stomach fluttering, I leap up and try pressing my feet in sets of two steps, side to side, against the linoleum floor, in the pattern taught to me by my friend and fellow performer, Martin Woods, an Inupiaq storyteller. I move my arms on either side of my body, like paddles in imagined seas. My left arm still doesn't stretch as far since my surgery, and I notice the careful movements of some of the elder Inuit women. I want to learn their stories.

We learned some dancing weeks ago in a workshop that Martin offered in our rehearsal room back in Juneau. Martin comes from Kotzebue, an Inuit village just above the Arctic Circle. It was there that Arctic Magic Flute first floated into my head, when I visited the village to teach classical European singing on a grant from the Alaskan School Boards. Ideas can be dangerous things. They rarely turn out exactly as expected. Ideas change everything, including us, if we let them.

On that starlit morning in 2005, the sharp sub-zero air stung my cheeks as I stepped from a single prop airplane onto the glittering tarmac. I'd arrived directly from business meetings in Anchorage, dressed in a skirt, tights and heels. My host, Anahma, and her mother, Linda, came to pick me up and shepherd me through the day.

Anahma took one look at me and laughed.

"You're going to want to change," she exclaimed.

After lunch, we went to the music room at the school where Linda teaches. While I got myself settled, a couple of students peeked in from volleyball practice, curious to see the "opera lady." Lois, a stately Inupiaq girl with a broad smile, leafed through some sheet music that we might sing at her lesson the next day. I tried to make a connection with her but couldn't get her to make eye contact. Anahma later explained that, in the Inupiat culture, averted eyes were a sign of respect and not disinterest. We all recognized that it was me who had the most to learn here.

Two years later, following our performance of Magic Flute in Kotzebue, Martin drummed and danced with young adults whom *he mentored. He taught us dances depicting hunting, fishing, and snow machine riding. His sister fed us caribou jerky, chewy muktuk dipped in pungent seal oil, and agutak (Inuit ice cream made with snow and berries).*

Martin taught my legs to pound the cold out of the earth, to pound the pain out of my heart. I learned humility and integrity. I learned how to be human.

This morning, we revel in the rare honor of dancing with esteemed elders from these scrappy islands between the Chukchi and Bering Seas. After taking turns sharing music with one another —ours written by Mozart and theirs by centuries of love and tenacity—we bounce and sway together, our arms cutting the electric air.

When talking to my husband about the book, particularly the section on "finding your people," Patrick wisely asked, "Just what do you mean by 'your people'? What are the criteria for choosing them?"

Excellent question. And. It's one of those experiences that's both simple and complicated to describe; you know it when you feel it. "Your people" may not look like, talk like, even think exactly like you. They will share "like-heartedness" with your values—people over profit; relationships in collaboration; elevating marginalized voices. We will increase the resilience and development of our movement only through personal integrity and diversity. There, I said it. The D word.

Our country's current (and terrible) campaign against "DEI" (and I would add "B" for Belonging) devalues and obscures the significance of diversity. Today's understanding of diversity is not what our parents or grandparents (or even ourselves) grew up spouting. True and abiding diversity does not happen in a "melting pot." Imagine taking all your crayons and melting them together. Yuck! Sounds like a big puddle of mess. Diversity looks more like a brilliant mosaic, tastes like a delicious, tossed salad. There is beautiful harmony, and some dissonance, yes, in this creative grouping, while each culture, each person, can be differentiated and authentic.

Also, this: we do not seek diversity to make everyone all cozy and self-righteous; that's just another form of colonizing! We movers seek diversity as an essential element to our own human evolution. Only by including and learning from all voices, particularly those marginalized outside of false norms, will we grow and move forward as a human race. It's a scientific fact!

It's also an artistic reality. As an opera singer, I know the exciting possibility of many distinct voices, singing different melodies and texts at the same time. It should sound like a mess, and yet it does not. It works! It's beautiful and moving. It's enormous!

A note on racism. Anti-acism shares a Venn diagram with diversity and yet addressing racism is a distinct, systemic topic. For more information on *How to Be an Antiracist* I highly recommend the book by that title by Ibram X. Kendi. Anti-racism is our moral obligation and one that supports the human evolution of nurturing diversity as a strength. It also intersects with interculturalism.

Intercultural communications, which are *not identical* to anti-racism, are skills that we can each and all build and develop. Honestly, I'm still working on mine. It helps to acknowledge that every communication in which we engage–with family, friends, colleagues, and strangers–is by its very nature intercultural. We each have our own unique cultural voices, the perspectives that make up our "suchness" (a wonderful term meaning "essential or characteristic quality"; used in the Buddhist practice of *tathata*). Just acknowledging this fact puts us on the path toward deep and meaningful diversity. Boom. Said it again!

Like any meaningful work, this takes time. Sadly, the push of capitalism often demands that we collaborate quickly, accomplishing our goal or project without taking the time to understand our context. While I've experienced and even driven this process many times before, now I ask: how can we respectfully collaborate without building community? How do we know where to stand in the choir when we don't know the voices of our fellow storytellers? And how can we collaborate fully without knowing and accepting the full spectrum of *our own* multiplicity of identities—our talents as well as fears, our scars along with our hopes?

One aim of our movement is joining our individual work on integrating our own lives with our process for collaborating with other like-hearted humans around shared interests. So, you might end up creating opera with folx in the Arctic (or not), or you might do something even more extraordinary. It depends on your clarity and your community.

In these next pages, now that we've rediscovered and ignited our own voices and passions, and before we embark on uniting with others to *Fill the Room* together, let's take a moment to consider how to collaborate, to integrate, *within ourselves.* Let's find harmony in our own brains and souls and then go forth to do so in community.

An Integrated Life

> "What we practice at a small scale can reverberate to the largest scale."
>
> — adrienne maree brown

Like most of you, I wear many hats, inhabit various roles (in my case, quite literally): wife and lover, mother, nanna, friend, singer, actor, runner, priest, writer, counselor, and coach. I've spent much of my adult life searching for a path that would allow me to integrate those roles, to feel that bone-deep authenticity of my full personhood in a project, a season, even in a moment. Those moments occurred rarely and fleetingly at first. Right now, I'm on a quest for it to happen more regularly and *sostenuto* (playing or singing in a manner that sustains each note to and beyond its full value).

We've discussed how the pressures of capitalism and specialization limit and discourage a fully integrated life. Another cause of our disintegrated identities can be even mildly traumatic memories that remain unprocessed and sequestered by our subconscious. Contemporary research and writing by authors such as Gabor Mattheo in Canada and Bessel VanDerKolk in the U.S. teaches us about how our brains fracture and store away painful experiences to help us keep surviving during difficult times.

Later, even though separate aspects of those memories may be stored in different areas of our brains, they may seep out indiscriminately and attach themselves to current experiences, which results in disproportionate, triggered responses to the present circumstance. A commonly referenced example is the combat veteran who hears fireworks and experiences an involuntary response in their body, one of sudden fear or anger. Something as

101

simple as a scent, a color, or a song can quickly transport us back to a memory we do not want to revisit, at a time and place when we are unprepared to revisit it. Also, when we remain fragmented and dissociated from our memories, we may inadvertently disconnect from important parts of our selves, even qualities and wisdom that we need to create and collaborate in the world.

As a small child, my earliest memories were of the farm where I lived as a toddler with my parents and aunt. Due to my mother's fearful experiences in that place, we suddenly moved to the suburbs, my earliest traumatic event. For years, I could not remember the pastoral setting, rich with trees, horses, and cows. As a result, for much of my adult life, I kept on moving, afraid to settle in or fall in love with any one place. Always waiting for the other shoe to drop. It wasn't until much later, with the help of a therapist, that I restored my affinity for green spaces and a rooted life. As I write this book, I'm gazing out at the trees and mountains of the Pacific Northwest once again and feel at home and fully present. The more we can heal, reframe, and reintegrate our experiences, the more fully available we can be for ourselves and others. After all: breaking down barriers, even in ourselves, opens the door for connection, doesn't it?

Over my years of study and practice, I've come to regard the act of growing up as a life-long process of integration. This integration includes not only childhood experiences from our families of origin and other relationships, but it also builds upon the culture from which we descend, including unresolved traumas buried within the decades, even centuries of that culture.

If you are BIPOC, you may be painfully familiar with this kind of generational trauma, and the way it can also form barriers to some of your generational strengths. Indigenous colleagues have explained to me how sharing their stories of abuse in residential schools, while both painful and healing, also liberates their connection to their Native culture, from which that trauma had intentionally separated them. When Phyllis Webstad, a third-generation residential school survivor, finally shared her story of abuse, framed by the symbol of a beloved orange shirt, she started the powerful movement of Orange Shirt Day. This celebration honoring survivors is now an important part of the Truth and Reconciliation process for Indigenous peoples in Canada.

The more we can understand, heal, and integrate our cultural identities, as we considered in the first movement of our journey, the greater our ability to heal our wounds, reframe our stories, and reclaim our resilience. From such a place of wholeness, we become better partners in collaboration.

Lifespan Integration

As someone who's experienced complex trauma throughout my life, I've engaged in various therapeutic methods over the years. Then I was introduced to a deeply transforming mode of therapy called Lifespan Integration (LI). LI began when, in 2012, psychotherapist Peggy Pace "synthesized the best of emerging forces" in therapy and brain science. Based on this emerging science and client centered practice, Pace developed protocols that enabled the "body and brain [to] believe that hardship has passed, and to [reorganize] into a more adaptive, higher level of function-ing."[1] In other words, becoming integrated helps us to heal and thrive.

Such integration in our lives begins and ends with our stories. In LI, the therapist outlines with each client a series of abbreviated timelines from their life, including their whole story, along with stories of relationships, or even briefer stories of distinct traumatic incidents. Using these timelines and engaging in some physical movements to connect to the body, care seekers begin to process

---

1.   Thorpe, Catherine , *Lifespan Integration,* pg. 3

their traumatic memories, previously stuck for years in fragments stored in different parts of their brain. This kind of process allows the care seekers to create new neuropathways, ones that reframe their story. Ones that say, "Then that happened. I survived. This is now. I'm loved."

This can extend to our own practices of expression–singing, writing, comedy (I see you, Hannah Gadsby!), visual art. By telling our stories with and alongside these creative practices, we may find a more profound and lasting release from our traumas, more than by telling our stories with words alone.

Note: Please, go gently into this next section, as it addresses traumatic memories. Make sure to have the support you need.

Have you ever experienced a moment when your own reaction to an event surprised you with its sudden vehemence? When you thought to yourself, "Wow! Where did *that* come from?" Chances are, the event you experienced triggered some part of your brain to recall a previous trauma, and your nervous system could not differentiate between then and now.

Take a moment and think about one such time. **For this exercise, please choose a memory or incident that has lost some of its rawness, that is not currently troubling you**. Do you have a gut feeling about what experience you may have recalled subconsciously? Write about it for a few minutes and allow yourself to be curious about its impact on your life. Bonus: what if you paint your story? Or sing it? Not for a gallery or concert hall. (Although, hey, if that's your jam, do it!) Even telling your story while out on a hike or run with a trusted friend can help to process things somatically. *Somatic*, from the Latin word *soma*, meaning body, recognizes the importance of whole-body awareness in the healing process. Consider looking up

Lifespan Integration practitioners in your area and explore possibilities with them. If you'd like to speak with me about this modality, I'd be honored to share with you what I've learned.

Telling our stories in an integrated way to those able to truly listen and witness can heal our lives. By extension, our healing heals the world. You know the saying, "Hurt people hurt people"? I believe that the opposite can also be true: healed people can heal people. And sometimes healing is uncomfortable.

Remember too, your transformation impacts the people in your life who are used to you behaving in certain habitual patterns. I've heard it explained like moving one piece of a mobile: it causes all the other pieces to wobble at first, and requires them to adjust and rebalance. Folx might not like it at first, or ever, *and that's ok.* They'll get over it; or not. That is their work to do. Not yours.

Our job is to first heal ourselves, and by doing so, provide more health and integration to systems around us. In this way we might begin healing the "ears" of the world, so that humans can *hear* many diverse stories in a new way and have the courage to accompany and amplify them. Stories from individual lives, and from generational and cultural experiences.

Sharing Our Stories and Culture

How often do you think about your culture in a day? Not only your genetic heritage–"my ancestors came here in the early 20th century, largely from Wales and Germany"–but also the cultural ground on which you stand, the air you breathe and how you breathe it, the waters in which you swim. Those of us who fall within the culturally dominant group may not initially recognize our culture as influencing how we view the world. Dominant culture presents itself as "normal" or "neutral" and then defines all other cultures in contrast to that norm.

We moved from Juneau, Alaska to Berkeley, California when

Ari was in first grade. One day that first fall when we picked her up from Malcolm X Elementary school, Ari began crying in the back seat of the car, completely crestfallen. When we asked her what was wrong, she burst out,

"Everyone else has a culture and I don't!" Wow. Such evolved thoughts developing inside that little, curly blonde head. Had we neglected this part of her education?

The next day, I began teaching Ari more about our Welsh roots. We learned a few words (not easy), sang several mournful songs (and less mournful lullabies), and told some family stories. This exploration extended for years, leading us all the way to visit her ancestors' row houses in Wales when she was 21.

Still, that first Berkeley winter, Ari insisted we celebrate Kwanzaa.

For me, my culture, my orientation includes being a white, straight, cisgender woman, past my child-bearing years, and still slogging it out in the middle class. I am a feminist, an advocate, and proud mother and grandmother of those with neurodiversity and queer identities. I grew up in the suburban U.S., was the first in my family to finish college, and had the privilege of traveling the world as a performer and then as clergy. All of that influences how I view things, how I speak, and how I am perceived. In short, my cultural voice. How about yours?

What are your stories of cultural ancestry? Do they fill you with pride and inspiration, or shame and grief, or a little of both? Take a moment and write about some of the ancestral, societal, racial and ethnic influences that create your voice–balancing honest awareness and self-compassion while doing so. Write down a story about a time you remember your voice–singing, writing, moving, creating art–reflecting and/or being judged by a cultural standard. Is there anything about your culture that inspires or heats up your expression? Consider speaking one of these stories to a human that you trust. Notice how that makes you feel.

My singing voice grew out of my Welsh roots. My paternal grandfather, Henry, came over on the proverbial "boat" as a pre-teen from southern Wales at the turn of the 20th century. During his childhood poverty, Grandpa scavenged the town for food and coal for his family and sang to the miners in pubs for coins. Henry himself mined for coal in his boyhood near his village of Bedlinog—ten minutes from the infamous Aberfan mine that killed 144 people, most of them children, when a landslide of slurry engulfed a primary school and a row of houses, like the ones in which he grew up, in 1966.

As a young girl, I listened hungrily to Grandpa's tales of fishing in the moats of castles. My little heart broke when he drank too much wine at dinner, grew quiet, and then told his childhood stories of friends dying right beside him down in the mines. And then I thrilled when he belted out a Celtic tune in his booming tenor, often summoning me to the head of the table where he would teach me to sing "from my gut," patting my little tummy and giving me a rudimentary idea of diaphragmatic breathing. By the age of 10, my voice grew more mature than my years (imagine a tiny July Andrews singing camp songs). A mixed blessing.

Grandpa took me to choral festivals in Seattle's Presbyterian churches, where I listened to massive men's choirs sing hymns in the Welsh language. He himself knew only a small bit of his native tongue—mostly words unfit for children—since at the time he grew up, the English government did not allow Welsh to be spoken. To this day, I keep near my piano the small hymn book with a red dragon on the cover, its precious pages filled with mysterious words and haunting tunes like the Welsh national anthem, and the beloved lullaby, Suo Gan ("All through the Night") that I sang to Ari.

During my life journey, I've become gradually more aware and skillful in recognizing the terrible impact that my ancestors' white privilege had upon people of color. Even as a child, I cringed at the racist slurs and attitudes expressed by my parents toward blacks in Seattle and Indigenous peoples in our hometown, and that shame gradually became determination and a quest for justice. I still have a way to go to reeducate myself, to remove the subconscious indoctrination of racism and colonialism. The place I begin this work is in understanding and speaking from my own culture. This enables me to better hear the stories of lives and cultures other than my own.

As we collaborate with other full and integrated voices, how can we do so in a non-colonizing way? How do we ask neither ourselves nor others to dim their light, to shrink their identities, and yet still create harmony together? I believe that we can begin to do so by knowing, developing, and acknowledging our own voices, our own culture. Fullness from fullness; integrity from integrity.

Building Cultural Bridges

One of the richest privileges of being a singer and storyteller is the opportunity to build bridges between cultures: between languages, classes, genders, and races. I've performed in French, German, Italian, Russian, and Spanish, with a bit of Tagalog and Swedish sprinkled in there. I've been honored to sing European American classical music, as well as historically black spirituals and jazz ballads, Russian folk songs, and newly composed music that mixes sounds from diverse cultures. I've sung in Germany and Switzerland, Trinidad and New England, Scotland and the Arctic, in bars and gymnasiums and mansions and drag shows and concert halls. Every occasion expanded my awareness about my own privilege, culture and voice.

One such time evolved out of the project funded by the Alaskan School Boards, whose story began this chapter/movement. A team of us traveled over the period of two years up to the

Arctic village of Kotzebue. We went there to create a new production of Mozart's *Magic Flute*. How can Mozart be new, you might ask? All you need is a fresh point of view, and tons of humility.

Owing to the spoken dialogue in *Die Zauberflote* (its German title)--a rarity in actual opera scores, though not in musicals--we were able to shift the narrative. After meeting with the Northwest Arctic Borough leadership and elders about the struggles and strengths of their community, director Ryan Conarro and I decided to transform this fantastical (and very problematic) tale of queens, enslaved humans, and princesses into a story of the urban/rural divide, one which resonated with many generations of Alaskan villagers.

Our Queen of the Night became the *Electric Queen*, the champion of all things modern; and instead of a Masonic grandmaster, Sarastro (Princess Pamina's dad) spoke as a village elder about the strong Native Alaskan values—sharing food, laughter, honoring elders and children —that saved their culture from peril. Pamina found herself torn between these two worlds and the outsider, Prince Tamino, needed to learn village ways to join Pamina in creating a new life.

We had many wise conversation partners in this project. Nature photographer and author Seth Kantner, a white settler living a subsistence life outside of the village from birth, became my cultural liaison. The beginnings were a bit rough.

"Are those Carhartts you have on?" Seth mused, scratching his beard, when he first met me in the local coffee shop.

"Yes," I bubbled, "they make them for women now, so they fit better. Never thought I'd wear them when I lived in New York." I laughed nervously.

Seth eyed me with suspicion, then advised,"You're going to want to give people a little space when you talk to them up here. Slow down. And back up and make some room for air between you. This isn't New York, you know, it's Kotzebue."

To fill that room, I needed a minute to understand my own identity and the context of the culture around me. I made lots of mistakes and learned as much about my own voice as about life in the Arctic. It was one of the hardest, most humbling things I've ever experienced, and one of the most satisfying. To find that balance between my strengths and others' without overshadowing any of us. At least, that was our goal.

This chapter's opening story describes the transformational honor of our meeting traditional dancers from the islands of Little Diomede and King Island. For years after evangelical missionaries colonized these tiny communities, Indigenous peoples were prohibited from dancing in their traditional style of storytelling. Typical of Anglocentric "conversions" at that time, these missionaries supposedly feared the evil spirits that might enter through such dancing.

Inupiaq dancers themselves already (and still) wore fur gloves during the dances, not out of fear of the Spirit, but out of respect. With dance they told stories of their history, their skills and traditions. Then, for decades, these stories remained untold, as their language and arts became forbidden.

When we visited the Arctic in 2007, the dances had only recently begun again. Now they depicted not only the stories of gathering food and paddling, but they also expressed what, for their ancestors, would have been the science fiction future of snow machine rides and airplane travel. The sacred stories of these wisdom bearers not only connected them to one another and their ancestors, they also offered a way for us visitors to connect with them, and to share some of our own stories.

On a bus ride one night to view the northern lights–that mysterious green curtain of the aurora borealis–I talked with an Indigenous woman about her history. When she explained how the abuse in residential schools created generational traumas for herself and others in the village, it helped me to understand how even stepping foot again through the doors of institutions like schools or churches, where we did most of our performing on tour, could trigger elders. She suggested we visit residents at the local Elder Home, where seniors were cared for with great respect.

"If you get some elders to come, everyone will come," she affirmed. And she was right.

When the time felt right, I ventured telling her my story about how my grandfather was beaten for speaking his native language in colonized Wales. Together, she and I discovered some of the folk tunes that were common between Celtic and Indigenous peoples, songs like *Waly Waly*, the Water is Wide, sung on the Trail of Tears by interracial couples of Indigenous people and Irish immigrants.

Later, as she and I stood side by side on a hill, we whistled together into the crystalline air, an Inuit tradition that is believed to make the lights dance. I'm not sure if it worked, or if our shivering, belly laughter just made it seem so, but it certainly blended our voices across the cosmos. We remembered our ancestors who sang and danced to keep remembering who they were. Now their songs connected us, their great-grandchildren, and on and on to the voices of our own children and grandchildren.

How about you? Do you know any of your ancestors' songs? Have you ever heard or read their stories? If you're lucky enough to still have living elders, ask them to tell you a story or sing a song. Write it down or ask them to record their voice to save as a treasure.

Then, consider learning about a culture other than your own by hearing and learning their dances, songs, stories. What might you learn? How might you build bridges? How might your voices create a new harmony together?

Building Solidarity in a Divided World

I've heard folx express so much frustration about the divisions in our world today, particularly in the U.S. Although I acknowledge that violence and injury often result from heated disagreements, sometimes I wonder if we aren't using that term "divisions" to gloss over oppression from the systems that divide us. Is there a way we can refocus this conversation to find new solutions? How can we create a just unity?

"Can't we all agree?" seems like a valid question, except I often hear it used to stifle the righteous grief and anger of those diminished by the current systems of capitalism, colonialism, and heterosexism. Twentieth century gay black author James Baldwin is attributed[2] as saying:

> We can disagree and still love each other unless your disagreement is rooted in my oppression and denial of my humanity and right to exist.

Victims of oppression and discrimination often get asked to forgive their abusers without an apology or any corresponding change in abusive behaviors. I'm not convinced that "going along" really helps us to get along; in the end, it helps those who hold greater power and allows oppressive and discriminatory beliefs to remain unchallenged for the sake of an unjust peace. Remember the words of Amanda Gorman: *"what just is, isn't always justice."*

What's more, marginalized groups are often pitted against one another, focusing the conversation on which group is more deserving of support. If I hear the phrase "women are their own worst enemies" one more time, I will puke. May we not speak–or

---

2. Gay black essayist and novelist Robert Jones Jr. writes under the moniker @sonofbaldwin, and leads to the frequent misattribution to Baldwin.

sing, write, dance, legislate–instead about what we can and will do and are doing *together* to change systems and expand boundaries? I'm there for that conversation.

As we approach the conclusion of our journey through this book, let's consider how to Fill the Room, together, with previously marginalized voices. And let's begin to explore which spaces we feel compelled to fill, and which must be filled with those whose voices have previously been excluded and silenced. Part of my, and hopefully our, core motivation for helping ostracized voices to rediscover their power, their light, their story, is to make an impact on the world at a time when the stakes could not be higher. Every voice is needed!

Even as I write, my queer and trans family and friends tremble at the terrors coming their way fast and furious since the 2024 presidential election. Every single day, on social media and in government actions, they find their very identity questioned and eradicated by the loud voices of misogynists in power. People of color, particularly Latinx folx and immigrants seeking refuge and opportunity in the U.S., now face being increasingly targeted, incarcerated without cause, and deported to the very places from which they fled. Women of reproductive age begin stocking up on needed contraceptive medicine as their sovereignty over their own bodies is threatened. Older women and BIPOC activists, who used their bravest voices decades ago to demand and deliver vital civil rights, now see their work begin to crumble and regress. We simply cannot let this happen, and we do not need to. We have the power, together, to sing a new song, to change the world with the collective resonance of our voices. Who's with me?

Creative Collaborations

In theatre, an important tool for performing, directing, or designing is focus. Focus. Where do we *focus* the light, or for purposes of this book, *our light?* When I work with younger actors, I first help grow their awareness of the power of their own light, within themselves. This is what you and I did together in the first two movements. Then the youth and I practice "shining our light" of focus on another actor. It feels good and right. In an ensemble, we can ask ourselves: whose voice needs to be heard, listened to, witnessed right here and now? And when one voice needs room to be heard, we focus the light on them. Next time you go to a play or watch a movie, notice the beauty in the person listening to, shining light on, another character. Gorgeous!

In a choir, when we sing the same vowel sound together, even with our different qualities of tone, the synced vibrations resound and grow, reverberating exponentially, disturbing the air, filling the room, more than even the sum of our voices when we are all operating without awareness of one another. To be clear: we don't need to all be the *same* voices, or to play small until our throats hurt, but rather be in concert with one another when we choose to be. Just so, in solidarity of focus and resonance, we will transform the space we're in.

As an extrovert, and a white, cisgender, straight, middle class woman of some privilege, I may feel more comfortable at times when called to speak hard truths in public spaces. I can also shine my light, my intention, my focus, on the voices of other feminists and humans of color, from a variety of locations, to create more space for us all. It just might work, y'all!

In her foundational book, *The Creative Connection: Expressive Arts as Healing,* pioneering psychotherapist Dr. Natalie Rogers explains how the creative process connects us not only to our inner selves, but to the community and the world.

As we first journey inward through the expressive arts, we tap into...new aspects of self, gaining insight and empowerment...by connecting to at least one other person...we learn

114

ways to relate to the community... We become co-creative and collaborative, being able to access our higher purpose and powers. This connects us to the world...with compassion.

Rogers concludes:

> As we change our consciousness, so will we change the world... to act constructively in the world, we need to broaden our consciousness to encompass the sufferings and joy of humankind and to find our connection to nature...Self-empowerment...translates into personal and social action.[3]

Sounds like a movement to me! Where shall we begin?

Your moment is now. This country is relying on each and every one of you to walk into your purpose and to walk in greatness with your head held high... And if nobody told you today—you are enough. You are ready. And you are needed.

— Jasmine Crockett, U.S. Representative

Which Spaces Shall We Fill?

According to a March 2025 study by the Pew Research Center,

---

3. Rogers, Natalie, *The Creative Connection: Expressive Arts as Healing*, Chapter 11

only 26% of the members of the U.S. Congress are people of color. While this number is up from 15% in 2005, it still does not represent the over 42% of ethnic minorities who comprise our country. Latinx lawmakers are especially underrepresented (11% of Congress vs. 20% of the U.S. population). 28% of the voting members of Congress are women, a figure unchanged from the previous year. Although increasing over the prior decade, women continue to make up a much smaller share of the federal legislature than of the U.S. population, which is 51% women.

Among queer folx, the number of legislative representatives is much, much smaller. Six members of the current Congress are gay men. Seven are lesbian, gay, transgender or queer women, according to data from the LGBTQ+ Victory Fund. Although these numbers have increased over the past decade, they have not grown since the previous year's Congress. And I very much fear they will decrease in the years ahead unless we speak out.

Pew Research also reports that the share of women CEOs of Fortune 500 companies reached an all-time high of a *whopping* (emphasis mine) 10.6% in 2023! Unacceptable. According to AboveBoard, "Fortune 500 diversity still has a long way to go to reach equity for underrepresented leaders."

Why is corporate diversity important? For one thing, since the Citizens United ruling gave corporations the same rights as individual humans, we need marginalized voices in that conglomerate. For another, as my late friend Dolly Oddi, an Italian immigrant from Boston, used to say, "Money talks, love's a whisper." I'm not saying that love isn't important or motivating, merely pointing out that money does have power (the ability to act).

Fortune 500 companies make up some two-thirds of the U.S. GDP, amounting to $18 trillion in revenues, according to Fortune in 2023. Yet, while "Black America's labor force participation rate is 13%", only 1.6% of Fortune Company CEOs are black; even fewer are Latinx, only one of which is a woman.[4] Only four out of 500 CEOs identify as LGBTQ+. *Four.* AboveBoard's takeaway is this: "change is happening, albeit slowly. And with the rollback of affirmative action, corporate diversity efforts are poised to face even more hurdles on the road to diversity, equity, and inclusion in the C-suite."

Where will we go from here? As the nation holds its breath in the wake of relentless government policies that increase the income inequality gap; demolish the values of diversity, equity, inclusion, and belonging; and withdraw support from disabled people, how can the combined voices of those on the margins move us forward into a more equitable future, rather than backward into another prejudiced and oppressive era?

Can we, as Rogers suggests, become empowered by the "sorrows and joys" of our stories and inspire one another to take "personal and social action"? I believe we can.

Mara's Story: The Power of Our Voices Together

When I was a teenager, I embarked into the world with full force. A thriving, energetic Korean adoptee with political aspirations to make the world a better place. I was full of life, ambition, and hope. If you asked me what I would do after graduation, I would have responded that I was going to change the Constitution so that I could be the first female president not born on US soil. My platform? To fight for equality and end discrimination.

My first real relationship not only dimmed my light, but it also landed me in therapy at the local women's shelter. My boyfriend "loved" me but was so uncomfortable in his own skin that I was soon conditioned not to be comfortable in mine. Highly empathetic, I began to take on his low self-esteem, and quickly learned to detest

---

4. US Bureau of Labor Statistics, February 2024

my body, question my mind, and foster conflict within myself. This eventually led to self-harming behaviors.

Despite the call of my inner nature and caring mentors, I began to make myself smaller, to become invisible, and to silence my voice; and all without much conscious effort. I quit all activities I enjoyed so I could shrink myself and make my boyfriend love me more. I began to question my life in this world and how I could belong in it.

After we broke up, I went to counseling and learned about abusive relationships. My parents, being actively engaged in the community, rallied so that people knew that I was healing and would embrace me in my recovery. I resumed my previous activities—competitive jump rope, student government, close friendships— and in addition I began voice lessons with Joyce.

Joyce inspired me, not only with the sounds that came out of her mouth and body, but also the unique way that she, as a feminist woman of privilege and advocacy, maintained the trust in herself she needed to heal herself and others. If you have ever taken voice lessons, you know that you can be invited to look in the mirror and make some odd feeling sounds and faces. You have full permission to be loud! You learn to be comfortable enough in your own skin so you can be completely goofy. You learn to surrender to the beauty in music as it rides on the energy of your own breath.

One stage of taking voice lessons can be picking a song and performing it solo in a recital. While I love to sing, I had not yet found the confidence to sing solo in front of other people. Nevertheless, Joyce believed in me. Together, we persisted and discovered a strength buried deep within my body. I experienced new comfort in using my muscles in tandem to lift the sound out of me and share it with others. Within my fear, I found my courage. Within my body, I found my voice.

The same year I was taking voice lessons, I ran for All Student Body President, and my campaign message was, "Claim your

Voice." Right!? *Representing my voice and the voices of others has been an integral part of my calling ever since.*

These early experiences opened my eyes to the oppression of the patriarchy—the system that puts men before women; one in which men have a voice, and women do not. So many times in my lifetime, the patriarchy told me I couldn't have a voice, that I didn't matter, that I should become invisible. And after you hear that message so often, it just becomes ingrained.

Despite this inner conflict, I ran for the city assembly when I was 23 years old. I went around to the politicians I knew to ask for their support. When the rest of the candidates threw their name in the ring, as the only young woman of color, they politely asked me not to run. Instead, the politicians in my community recruited a much older white male to run in the race because they believed he would have more success winning.

I refused to bow out since I had already put my name forward. I held my own and I proved to be a contender, despite ultimately losing the race. When I needed to learn the details of the issues in our community, I met with leaders in our town. The predominantly white male leaders I met would most often tell me things they assumed I didn't know, and I smiled and played along. As a young woman, I'd learned to survive by not letting on how much knowledge I possessed. I thought that playing small kept me safe.

In my late 20s, I taught English in South Korea. My husband at the time insisted this was something we should do before settling down and starting a family. The Confucianist principles of hierarchy in the Korean education system stifled me so much that I did not complete my 12-month contract. Meanwhile, my Caucasian husband reaped all the benefits of male supremacy, while I simply did not exist. The lesson again: men took up space, women stayed small.

Heartbreakingly, the cycle of abuse continued in my life, eventually witnessed by my two young children. The unspoken expecta-

tions of motherhood complicated things further, with its stereotypes of selfless servitude. Nonetheless, in December of 2022, I found the courage to file a domestic violence protective order and ended the marriage.

As I healed from my trauma and unpacked the dynamics of that unhealthy relationship, I saw the same old story. A partner with low self-esteem threatened by a strong woman who shrinks herself to survive, convinced by toxic masculinity that he must be bigger and reacting with abuse and violence when he felt insecure.

How could I have let this happen again? How did I not act sooner when I saw so many red flags? Conditioned from childhood to accept, to smile, to please, women (especially women of color, and those of Asian culture) learn to take on the shame and blame that keeps us oppressed. Yet, as I shared my story in community, I awakened to how many other women hid stories like mine. The more I spoke about my experience, the more women felt comfortable to be present with theirs.

In 2023, part of my healing journey was to take a self-defense class. I wanted to learn to protect myself and my children and never wanted to find myself in a position where I passively witnessed violence in my home ever again. That self-defense class grew into Judo classes.

With Judo, I unlearned the thinking in which women are conditioned from the beginning of our lives: unlearned the politeness, unlearned playing small, unlearned taking up less space, unlearned apologizing for simply existing. Once again, I found my courage through doing something completely awkward and terrifying on a weekly basis. What seemed impossible gradually became my reality. Like my voice lessons with more action!

Around the same time, I also began fire breathing meditation and somatic release through a women's workout called Airbar Fit. One of the parallels between voice study, Judo, and Airbar Fit is *that to tap into your physical strength, you connect by making vocal sounds. The voice activates your strength and directly connects to your power. I rediscovered my powerful voice deep within myself. These practices built upon the mind-body connection that I learned studying with Joyce: working with the energy that exists within me, both physically and mentally, and harnessing that connection to act with power in my life.*

I still struggle to continue processing my lifelong fear. The gaslighting from myself, my partner, and society all make me question my reality daily. If women share our stories, it can often be accompanied by fear, questioning, shame, and doubt. And.

The voice I carry now fights for who I am and what I believe in. The voice I carry now advocates for my child with special needs. The voice I carry now supports my aging and cognitively impaired parents. My voice is my power, and not only do I use it for myself, I use it to protect those nearest and dearest to my heart and those impacted by oppression.

Patriarchy may have crushed me in the past, but with support and mentorship, it also pushed me to rediscover my strongest, most authentic self and share my story to uplift others. Together we can build our courage and speak our truths, Fill the Room, and rise.

Finding Your Peeps

Ok. Now that you've dusted off, cherished, and expanded your authentic, beautiful, powerful voice, heard stories of transformation, considered ways to integrate parts of your own identity, and read just some of the hard facts about the need for solidarity among like-hearted revolutionaries, where do you find "your people"? How do you connect with groups and organizations that work together in ways that are mutually empowering rather than colonizing, and contribute your gifts and experiences to the movement ahead?

Start with your Sorrow and your Joys

Fill the Room, and any movement not powered by what some term "toxic positivity" or in the faith world, "prosperity Gospel," does not ask you to deny your struggles and pain. We will never say "there but for the grace of G*d"–everyone deserves grace, no exceptions. Suffering is not a sign of a lack of blessings; neither is abundance reserved for particularly "blessed" (read: privileged) people. On the contrary, I believe that our wounds can be a powerful source of healing, for ourselves and for others.

Author and theologian Henri Nouwen wrote in his book *The Wounded Healer:*

> When we become aware that we do not have to escape our pains, but that we can mobilize them into a common search for life, those very pains are transformed from expressions of despair into signs of hope. Nobody escapes being wounded. We are all wounded people, whether physically, emotionally, mentally, or spiritually. The main question is not "How can we hide our wounds?" so we don't have to be embarrassed but "How can we put our woundedness in the service of others?" When our wounds cease to be a source of shame and become a source of healing, we have become wounded healers.

For the past 20 years, my family and I have accompanied one of our own who lives with a diagnosis of mental illness. As someone who has done hard things, I'll tell you true: this has been the hardest. During seminary, I took a class outside our curriculum: the "Family to Family" course offered by NAMI (the National Alliance on Mental Illness) saved our lives, through empowering knowledge and resources, and most importantly by connecting us with other families on a similar journey. At NAMI we identified three phases on our cyclical journey: we could be in crisis, in stasis, or in advocacy. We might move from one phase to another with lightning speed. Good news: we were no longer alone. Now that my family member has found their path to healing, I still advocate for this cause, one increasingly underfunded and underserved, while at the same time over-stigmatized in Western society.

What cause is close to your life, close to your pain? Domestic violence? Poverty and food insecurity? Civil rights? Take a moment for a clear, appreciative look at the wounds in your life and recognize the resilience they represent, as well as the call to promote healing.

Then do some research. Go out and talk to those you love and respect about their experiences with these kinds of sorrows. How did they find strength? What groups helped them to continue forward? Take some time to visit groups you identify in conversations or online searches. If it's not a perfect fit, that's ok. As my own life coach, Rev. Dr. Scott Stoner, reminds me regularly, "Don't let the perfect be the enemy of the good." Process, not perfection, y'all.

If you're already associated with groups advocating for a wound close to your heart through donations, membership, or special events, consider stepping forward a bit more. What other investments can you make, in time and leadership? How can you connect with these people and causes with your newly rediscovered and strengthened voice?

Let's not forget the power of joy. Frequently, someone will mishear my name and call me "Joy," and it always brightens my day! What passions and happiness have you experienced on this journey to follow your calling? Have you felt elated by singing? Consider joining a local choir, particularly one that advocates for empowerment and community action. Did drawing or painting set your soul on fire? How about creating pieces that represent the values for which you'd like to advocate? Are there groups of other artists doing work to support those values? Find a performance group devoted to changing unjust systems and contribute your voice as a performer, designer, on the board, or in publicity. Maybe it's gardening, climate change, building things, creating housing, or cooking or feeding people. When you listen to your call, I pinky-promise that opportunities for connection will follow.

Here's another promise. The results of listening to your call might—hell, probably will—scare you. Rather than running in the opposite direction, consider your fear as an important sign that you're moving where you need to go.

Run for public office. Yup, you heard that right. I'm not saying run for president (but I'm not NOT saying it), but how about city council? Mayor? State representative? You read those statistics—we need your voice! If that's too much right now, how about volunteering on someone else's campaign, someone else on the margins who you believe in? Or even volunteering to get out the vote? Or participating in one of the many, many marches around the country right now, as an organizer, sign painter, or just peopling the bullhorn with your gorgeous pipes. Take a course on community organizing. If you belong to a faith background, I invite you to investigate the Gamaliel network (the organization that trained Barack Obama) and see what they offer in your area.

You can also start smaller. A regular coffee discussion among women of color interested in consolidating their power? Yes please! Cocktails (and mocktails) with fellow queer folx to talk about your lives and how you can feel safer? Sounds good. An online chat with folx living with disability about the current changes to policies and what you can do about it? I'm there for that. And let me know how I can help you *Fill the Room*. I'm down for working with you, one on one or with your group. Tell me, or another mentor, what you need. Creative ideas make us stronger, together. Rising tides, my friends.

Some Ideas

As we begin this movement, together, my mind and heart overflow with ideas for ways and locations for us to gather and collaborate ("collude" is the verb many of my organizer friends like to use, and it makes me giggle). Read on and make a note of ideas that come up in your own brain bubble so you can pass them on!

Online Seminars

Yes, I know, during the pandemic years, I too developed an aversion to Zoom gatherings. And yet, I also realized that this tool provides a meeting place for busy people living far apart. Visit our website at joyceparrymoore.com to locate and sign up for the next "Fill the *Zoom*" session. (See what I did there?) We will curate groups and topics, creating a safe and supportive environment for sharing stories and shining light on other voices.

In-Person Retreats

If you became inspired to visit (or revisit) any of the places mentioned in these pages–Ireland, Scotland, California, Alaska, British Columbia–let me know! Stay tuned for multi-day retreats convened in breath-giving locations around the world. Imagine using your voice to *Fill the Abbey* on the Island of Iona; or sharing stories and folk songs on the wee Irish island of Inis Mòr; perhaps journaling and painting together after a hike in the rainforests of southeast Alaska. The world is our "moveable feast" (thanks Hemingway), where we can nourish our souls and forge new partnerships on our way to creating change together.

FTR: The Gathering

Already have a group that meets to collude (tee hee) together? Invite me, along with some of my colleagues, to gather with you. Share your stories, goals, and fears, and *Fill the Room* will accompany you and encourage you on your journey toward fullness. Whether it's at your church, conference, synagogue, book group, running group, you name it, the more of us working together, the more spaces we can fill with light and creativity and transformational power.

Fill the Room Choirs

Of course! Seems like a natural, doesn't it? Would you like to help form a group of voices—those who have experienced marginalization, and who want to literally fill the room with their singing—to create and share vocal pieces that inspire others to step out of the shadows, to stop playing small, and to experience the magic of group resonance? Let's do it!

My background and contacts in vocal music can help your group choose pieces that facilitate healing, to challenge and motivate your choir. You can even invite me for a rehearsal to coach you and help cross-promote your events. For that matter, we can "harmonize" our strengths in other types of choirs: a symphony of storytellers; a chorus of comics; a madrigal of movement. Stay tuned for a list of values that can qualify your group as a *Fill the Room* affiliate choir.

Networking

Have you heard the African proverb, "If you want to go fast, go alone; if you want to go far, go together"? Of course, there's nothing wrong with moving fast or alone, if that's what you're able to do right now. And. We will move further and in a more lasting way if we move together.

That's the goal directing the three movements of this book– first, to rediscover and heal your own powerful, creative, innova- tive voice; second, to learn new methods and enlist new mentors to help you develop and strengthen your voice; and third (and this is the point here), to reach out with that voice to connect with others and create lasting change.

When I underwent chemotherapy and radiation treatments for breast cancer, I belonged to a running group called Team Survivor, in Juneau, Alaska. We supported one another on each stage of our path: diagnosis, treatment, struggle, and survival. We passed along our knowledge and stories to encourage one another and walked together along the way. We even ran an actual relay "race" together. (I frame the word with quotations because, for most of us, our version of "winning" was finishing! Our motto was "We may be slow, but we're loud!") The Klondike Road Relay traversed 100 miles between Skagway, Alaska and Whitehorse, Yukon, in ten legs of varying lengths and difficulty.

Leg 1 started out on the streets of the historic gold-mining town of Skagway, near the Red Onion Saloon; leg 2 was short, but nearly straight up, inclining to reach the mountain terrain; leg 3 we dubbed the "princess leg," since it was the shortest and flattest, reserved on our team of survivors for those most recently completing their treatments. We each had our portion to run and supported our teammates as they ran theirs. No comparison, no competition, just solidarity.

I first joined this team as a supporter, having not yet been diagnosed. When I received my diagnosis, years later, my teammates were the first ones I contacted for support. Throughout this difficult journey, and in many other periods of resilience since, I remembered in my soul and my body how it felt to run for miles in the dark, up and down hills, knowing that a group of caterwauling women drove just ahead of me with sustenance and cheers.

How can we serve as "support vehicles" for others? By promoting their projects and businesses? By sharing our tips and successes in whatever spaces we fill? By disseminating information on important protests and legislative initiatives? Just by being there for them when they need a rest and a drink of water? Telling a joke when they need a laugh? My hope and intention for this book, this practice, this movement is that it will provide support for marginalized voices and a means to network and connect whenever possible.

What's next?

Once again, let's celebrate how far we've come. First, you opened a book with a surprising and maybe intimidating title. *Fill the Room?* That's not allowed, is it? An invitation to take up space? There's got to be a catch. Will we get in trouble for this?

Yet, you persisted, taking time to listen for, differentiate and dust off your *vox, voce, vocation*. You took a serious look at the boxes that have held your voice, your body, your identity captive, perhaps for years, and thought about how to dismantle or abandon them for greener pastures. You acknowledged the power in your voice, and that power can be a good thing, available to everyone, as the ability to act.

And just now, we began considering all the ways we can locate and collaborate with an expanding list of people. We've imagined the places in which we can collaborate, in solidarity, to keep this party going, include more marginalized voices, and build momentum. Is that it? Done? Not quite yet, dear revolutionary.

Like most important explorations of life–physics, astronomy, climate, psychology–this journey of discovery, development, and collaboration runs in a cycle, repeating itself over again. Rather than thinking of it as a two-dimensional circle, where we seem to end up in the same place each go around, I imagine this cycle as a spiral staircase, winding its way around and upward, gaining new attitudes of perspective along the way.

As with all great pursuits, we begin where we are, right now. Perhaps you've already done deep work to articulate your voice and your calling and seek resources and people to help you take the next steps. Brava! Or you're feeling strong enough now to jump into collaborating. Go for it! If you're the innovator I think you are, you may balk at this sequence of things, and want to engage in discovery, development, and collaboration all at once. Good on you! There is no one right way. Believing that there is, friends, well, that's the beginning of colonialism, isn't it? We've had quite enough of that, thank you!

Part of hearing your voice means trusting what you hear and following that instinct. Are you in the thick of a vocation that once felt right, and now are sensing the urge to reexamine and perhaps course correct your original impulse? We're there for you. Even if you discover that you just want to reframe what it is you're doing, that's enough. Because you are enough.

Don't forget, sometimes we stumble. Lord knows, I do. Sometimes we trip and fall. Heck, sometimes we crash and burn, or are even pushed down the stairs! And it hurts like a sonofabitch. That's when it's great to return to practice, like consulting our inner physician, to help us right ourselves and get moving again. It's also so comforting to have a squad of folx to help pick you up and dust you off after you're down. This is a no shame zone, remember? As Brené Brown says, "Courage starts with showing up and letting ourselves be seen." I see you.

Wherever you are right now, you have the courage, the resilience, the support you need to be ok. Better than ok! To beautifully, authentically, powerfully take up space. To move forward. We are all rooting for you. Onward and upward!

Coda

CODA: A passage that concludes a piece (or a movement). From the Latin "cauda" meaning tail, edge, or trail. It may be as simple as a few measures, or as complex as an entire section. It has an impact on the meaning of the piece to the listener.

If you can't fly then run, if you can't run then walk, if you can't walk then crawl, but whatever you do you have to keep moving forward.

— Martin Luther King Jr.

HER BREATH EXPANDS DEEP INTO HER BELLY, PULLED FROM THE *energy under her feet, up through the stone floor, from the earth beneath. Harp-like notes cascade from the shining, black baby grand. Her dear friend, another goddess, coaxes the melody from the* keys with gentle assurance. Opening her lips, the diva arches her soft palate, enlarging the cave of her mouth above her low and relaxed larynx, grounded in peace and the sureness of her own body. In a moment, her vision of the phrase will manifest itself in her being, vibrating in her throat, head, belly, bones, filling the room, and disturbing the air with meaning.

"Oh Moon, do not fail me!" The words in Czech originate from folk tales, from sea and sky, intersecting with her own story of loss and love. They reach out to connect with the hearts of those gathered. The vibration begins with the "mmmm" of Miesichku, "moon" in Czech, until it blossoms into something bigger than her, larger than all of them. They're mutually invested.

The aria carries more than anyone can express: lifetimes of struggle, years of being told they were too much, or too little; the fractures of trauma-created wounds that, like Japanese pottery, healed and shine with gold. She contains multitudes, standing in all her elements: a priestess, in a holy place, at the altar of the piano, accompanied by a talented friend, another woman, a mother, one who'd been taught to speak softly, herself harboring streams of inner laughter and wisdom. The women behold one another, feeling the shift in how things will be.

An unspoken rightness permeates the room. All she had ever been and done fills her sea-green gown, now stretching tighter, proudly outlining her post-menopausal curves. The judgements and limitations placed on her by other voices—professors, teachers, parents, and patriarchal culture—slough off like scales. She sees clearly.

When the singing stops, they savor the lingering vibration for a moment longer, grateful for the space filled with pure possibility. The integration of story and technique and experience and study inspires them as one body. They hesitate to break the silence, so pregnant with surprise, with affirmation. If this could happen, then *what? They hold that question in their collective hearts, memorizing it, letting it ignite a spark within them.*

"What if," they wonder. What if they could shatter boundaries together, their collective voices surpassing what they could ask or imagine? How will they each find such a place in themselves, a place that draws from the air and soil, from their own creative nature? Reaching back to their ancestors for courage and inspiration, and toward the future with a force beyond their individual selves, beyond the room, beyond. What then? They hold the moment a bit longer, not moving, until at last, applause erupts and breaks the spell.

Begin and begin again

I wrote this book during a challenging transition in my life. After devoting 20 years to becoming and serving as an Episcopal/Anglican priest in a settled parish, I said "when." Over the past few years, it became increasingly clear that my call was leading me beyond the narrow confines of an institution. This realization prompted a movement in my own life, not only to retire as a parish priest, but to examine my body of work, my education in voice, teaching, theology, counseling, and coaching, and to imagine a new path, a new way.

This transition, as with most in-between places, tested me and purified me like a white-hot flame. There were days when just getting out of bed seemed a bit much. And each time I managed to make it to my laptop (read: typewriter, thank you Rev. Murray) my vision cleared, my voice became strong again, and the way began to open.

I share this now, here, at the conclusion of our reading time together on the off chance that just such a challenging transition led you to these pages. I want you to feel, among other things, hopeful, motivated, and supported. Like a master (mistress?) piece evolving. Right now, right this second, many, many people in your life love you, believe in you, and are ready to be part of your squad, perhaps even to join your movement. As Rachel Rogers[1] writes, "the impossible only seems that way until it happens."

The reason I want you to find, strengthen, and use your voice is not just for me and my coaching business (although I'd be honored to accompany you on your quest); it's not even for you alone, although I'm thrilled to see how you will grow and what you will accomplish with others. This book exists because *the world needs your voice right now*. Truly. I believe this and hope that by this point, you believe it too.

Our human development continues from our first breath until our last (and perhaps beyond). We develop within the context of our families, our communities, and the structures of our society and culture. Remember what we acknowledged in the first several pages of our conversation: that those of us in marginalized demographics receive countless messages all day every day telling us to be smaller, take up less space, play by the rules, to fit in and to blend. As we conclude our first dialogue with one another, may we re-*member* (literally put ourselves back together) that these diminutive ideals benefit only those who oppress us. We are told to play small by those "in charge," for fear that the power of our collective voices–*as we are*–can spark transformation in a suffering world. Yet, those in a dominant demographic may not realize that such fear hurts them, too. Becoming our true selves, singing our songs of the genuine, benefits everyone. Period.

Our becoming happens not only on our own, but with community. We become together.

---

1. Homepage - Rachel Rodgers

Sheldon's Story: Moving Together toward Becoming

At what point do we set a course toward becoming who we are? That is to say, who we want to be. A lot of folks face difficult obstacles on that journey. I was lucky enough to find music, and performing arts, early in my life. My voice gave me a voice. I love sharing beautiful sounds.

It's so interesting to me that music is simply sound. As we develop proficiency in making those sounds, we discover their meaning. They evoke an emotion. Sometimes, human language is added, and we're lifted to another level. Fascinating! I have been able to connect with so many others using this visceral form of communication.

At first, I merely shared music with friends for fun. Later, as I learned the "why" of music—the reason composers wrote what they wrote, the times in history certain pieces were written, and what it all meant to people, and communities—he importance of it became huge. I give credit to all the teachers and friends along my path who guided and shaped my learning. And I recognize the ways that music kept me safe.

My family lived in Great Falls, Montana during Junior High, because my father was stationed there in the Air Force. On the Air Force Base, there were many types of people. Outside of the Base, in the town of Great Falls, I was treated differently. Mainly because we were a black family in a traditionally non-black part of the country. It wasn't overtly hostile, but uncomfortable at times.

At school, I found that singing in the chorus helped me to connect with people. In that atmosphere we seemed to overlook or overcome our differences. Was music magic? I'd like to think so. At least we communicated with open hearts. I'm happy to say that the musical journey continued when my family moved to Tacoma, Washington. There, I was closer to metropolitan areas, arts, and ideas. I got to study with teachers such as Pamela LaSalle at Seattle Opera and my mentor, Bruce Pullan, at Western Washington University. I met wonderful, lifelong friends who were on similar paths to mine. We shared immense and transforming joy.

That's how I met Joyce (then Parry), my bubbly, soprano bestie, now The Rev. Dr. Parry-Moore. Joyce and I spent so many days and years performing together, in choirs and musical theatre, and sharing life's joys and sorrows. Our knowledge of one another has developed over the years into the kind of friendship that I wish everyone could have. Joyce became a sister, with an unbreakable bond of many years. (That's funny, since we're both still so young!) A bond forged through our voices.

An essential moment on my life journey was coming out as a proud gay man. The arts provided a safe space for me to grow and learn about myself. It is not lost on me that queer folx outside of the arts may not always feel so safe in their lives. Being fortunate enough not to have experienced insurmountable obstacles in my own life gave me the courage to live proudly as myself, and the ability to support others in their struggles.

One of the most inspirational moments in my life was performing in the Broadway show, Ragtime. *This powerful piece documents the transformation of society's attitudes at the turn of the last century. Slowly, and sometimes painfully, white, male, hetero-normative humans and systems began to accept others. African Americans, Jews, and women demanded their voices be heard. That was over a century ago, and lately we seem to be slipping backward. Our voices are still needed!*

Today, I feel lucky and grateful to be a member of the Gay Men's Chorus of Los Angeles. This organization uses music to promote the visibility and inclusion of voices that still need help to be heard. The chorus reaches out to many parts of the community. We work with churches, schools, and major arts organizations in California to amplify a message of strength and inclusion. All of this is done through music. Music. The art of sound still helps to shape the world. It's up to us all to welcome enough people into the room and to keep it resonating with the sound of hope.

So, what's next?

What will be your next movement in this sonata of transformation? What sound, what song of hope will you sing, write, dance, speak, teach, legislate?

For some of you, reading (and rereading) this book may be just exactly what you can do right now and that's great! Talk about it, practice on your own, place it in your "toolbelt" so it will be there for you when you need it to solve a problem and co-create a solution.

For others of you, these ideas may simply give you a taste for the nourishment you've been craving all along. How and where can you satisfy that hunger? Here are a few ideas.

You can consider taking vocal coaching. *Wait, hear me out!* Find a gentle, non-colonizing guide, someone who can honor the sound in you, and help you to free your authentic voice and use it in ways you hadn't yet thought possible. You can find a coach online, or at a school or university. Fill the Room Coaching offers vocal coaching in person and online, in keeping with the values of this book, this movement. Reach out through our website.

You can engage in life coaching. We've considered how many areas of voice and life overlap and inform one another. A life coach will accompany you along the path to identify, clarify, integrate, and achieve your life goals. This may look like a transformation in your career, or a change in an important relationship or family dynamic. You may find yourself living like the person you've dreamed of becoming. Most life coaches offer some kind of free introductory consultation, to determine a match of your styles and values. Then you can schedule a handful of sessions and take it from there. A coaching relationship may last for months, years, or become a resource to dip in and out of throughout the rest of your lifetime. You decide.

Finally, you might consider spiritual coaching. Wounds inflicted by faith systems and leaders can be highly traumatic and difficult to heal; likewise, the theology (your philosophy of your human and spiritual life) that leads to such wounding also needs re-framing. If you're not feeling safe in a faith community now, or even if you're part of a community you enjoy, and still seek something deeper, a coach or spiritual director can help. My education as a pastoral counselor in interfaith and intercultural settings may offer a bridge in your road to spiritual health.

With *Fill the Room*, I offer a somatic (physical, mental and spiritual) approach that can help you heal from toxic beliefs and past traumas, and rewrite your own powerful and integrated narrative, your "song." Then I can help you to "sing" it, whether literally or figuratively. Again, explore my website and send me a shout. I can't wait to hear your voice!

Finally, a guarantee: the more you use your voice, the more like-hearted people will gather around you. Resonance finds resonance. Whether you find solidarity in an activist group, a service organization, a sports team (dragon boats, anyone?), perhaps a choir or even (gasp!) opera or theatre company, discovering and strengthening your own identity and voice switches on the light in you that attracts others with a similar calling. I'm so excited for you!

Whatever happens, stay true, keep taking up space, keep making your own powerful, beautiful, fierce, healing sound. Know that you are just exactly who you need to be, and that you are worthy of filling rooms, streets, and buildings with the glorious light that is you. You are enough. You are beloved. You are not alone.

Let's hear you roar!

With love, blessings, and confidence,
Doctor Joyce

Some Resources for further exploration

Here's just a partial list of books that may help you in your journey, as they have in mine.

- Bogart, Anne, *What's the Story: Essays about Art, Theatre, and Storytelling,* New York, 2014
- brown, adrienne maree, *Emergent Strategy: shaping change, changing worlds*, Chico, CA 2017
- hooks, bell, *Teaching to Transgress: Education as the Practice of Freedom*, New York, 1994
- Kendi, Ibram X., *How to be an Antiracist,* New York, 2019
- Newell, J. Philip, *Listening for the Heartbeat of God: A Celtic Spirituality,* New York, 1997
- O'Donohue, John, *Beauty, the Invisible Embrace,* Great Britain, 2003
- Palmer, Parker, *Let your Life Speak: Listening for the Voice of Vocation,* San Francisco, 2002
- Rogers, Natalie, *The Creative Connection: Expressive Arts as Healing*,Palo Alto, CA 1993
- Thurman, Howard, *Jesus and the Disinherited,* Boston, 1976
- Vaid-Menon, Alok, *Beyond the Gender Binary,* Pocket Change Collective, 2021
- Van Der Kolk, Bessel, *The Body Keeps the Score, Brain, Mind, and Body in the Healing of Trauma*, New York City, 2014